A PHOTOGRAPHIC GUIDE TO

BIRDS
OF
SRI LANKA

GEHAN DE SILVA WIJEYERATNE, DEEPAL WARAKAGODA *and* T.S.U. DE ZYLVA

D1393388

Reprinted in 2008
First published in 2000 by
New Holland Publishers (UK) Ltd
London • Cape Town • Sydney • Auckland

Garfield House   80 McKenzie Street
86-88 Edgware Road   Cape Town 8001
London W2 2EA   South Africa
United Kingdom
www.newhollandpublishers.com

14 Aquatic Drive   218 Lake Road
Frenchs Forest   Northcote
NSW 2086   Auckland
Australia   New Zealand

ISBN 978 1 85974 511 3

Publishing Manager/Commissioning Editor: Jo Hemmings
Editors: Tony Stones and Bob Watts
Project Editor: Michaella Standen
Design and cartography: D & N Publishing, Hungerford, Berkshire
Production Controller: Joan Woodroffe

Reproduction by Modern Age Repro House Limited, Hong Kong
Printed and bound in Malaysia by Times Offset (M) Sdn Bhd

10 9 8 7

Front cover photograph: Sri Lanka Blue Magpie (T.S.U. de Zylva)
Title page photograph: Oriental Dwarf Kingfisher (T.S.U. de Zylva)

Acknowledgements
Thanks to Steve Rooke who introduced Gehan and Deepal to Jo Hemmings.
Thanks to Jo, Michaella Standen and other New Holland staff who have
worked on this book. Gehan thanks Dr. T.S.U. and Deepal for accepting the
invitation to participate in the book. Many photographers responded
promptly to fill in the gaps in the picture list. Vijita de Silva helped with preliminary proof-reading and Lester Perera provided logistical support in the
field. Kithsiri Gunawardena assisted with the transcription of some of the
songs and calls. Yu Es helped in various ways. Nirma and Damayanthi tol-
erated absences from home and abstinence from parental duties while Gehan
and Deepal worked on the book. Upamali has been a source of inspiration
and encouragement to T.S.U.

Contents

Introduction

Sri Lanka is a birdwatching destination with much to offer. A good network of roads and national parks combined with a good infrastructure for tourism place the 26 endemics within easy reach of birders. Dedicated birders will spend most of their time in the wet lowlands and the highlands where the endemics are concentrated. But there is much for the casual birdwatcher throughout the country. There is still enough forest cover around the major archaeological sites for a family on a general tour to combine birdwatching with culture. Over 100 species of Indian sub-continental birds can be seen, for example, in the environs of the cultural cities of Anuradhapura and Polonnaruwa.

Who should read this book?

A pocket guide such as this suffers from the inevitable restrictions of space in order to make it pocket sized. Most birds covered here are those likely to be seen by a visitor on a short tour, or by residents with a casual interest in birds. However, due to the difficulty of sourcing adequate photographs, we have included a few rare migrants as well. 'Birders' (hardcore birdwatchers) are more likely to use one of the comprehensive field guides and be on a bespoke tour. However birders on a family holiday with less time for birding may find a compact guide such as this easier to carry around. To meet their needs clues are given or brief descriptions are included in the text on separating similar looking species. In particular, attention has also been drawn to endemics and potential endemics which are likely to be of interest.

The climatic zones

Topographically, Sri Lanka can be described as comprising three peneplains or erosion levels. The lowest level, from 0-30 m forms the coastline and much of the north-central plains. This encircles a hilly centre in the southern half formed of a second peneplain rising to 480m and a third higher peneplain rising to 1,800m. The central hills are an obstacle to the path of the two monsoons causing them to shed rain. The northeast monsoon occurs between October and January bringing rain mostly to the northeast, and the southwest monsoon brings rain between May and August to the southwest. Some parts of the hills receive rain from both monsoons. The Peak Wilderness Sanctuary in the hills has been described as 'the most constantly wet part of Asia west of Borneo'. The combination of rainfall and topography have resulted in climatic zones supporting races of animals confined to a particular zone. Broadly speaking, the zones are divided into the dry zone comprising the coastal areas in the north, east, south and the north central parts of the country, and the wet zone comprising the west and the hilly central massif.

The wet zone could be further sub divided into the low, mid and high elevations. The wet zone is where much of Sri Lanka's biodiversity is concentrated. Despite a long tradition of natural history study, species await description even amongst the higher animals such as small mammals, reptiles and amphibians. Some of Sri Lanka's endemic species probably vanished before science could even describe them as the hill forests were cleared in the 19th century for coffee. It is unlikely that any more species of birds await discovery, but further studies may see the elevation of some subspecies to full species status.

The avifauna of Sri Lanka

The island has 233 resident species of which 26 are recognised as endemic by the Ceylon Bird Club. The bulk of the resident species are shared with the Asian mainland, with a few confined to Sri Lanka and the Indian mainland. A few resident birds have a cosmopolitan world distribution. A further 198 species have been recorded as migrants to the country. The majority of these migrate to Sri Lanka during the northern winter and are present from about August to April. In contrast, pelagic species of seabirds like Shearwaters, Petrels, Storm-Petrels etc. migrate to Sri Lankan waters from southern oceanic islands during the southern hemisphere's winter. Of the migrants, about 100 species regularly visit the country. The rest are occasional visitors and vagrants.

Within the country, some species are distributed according to the climatic zones, being restricted to either the wet or dry zone. The endemics are largely confined to the wet zone. The distribution of birds is also influenced by altitude and some species may be restricted to the low country wet zone with others confined to the montane wet zone. In total, the Sri Lankan avifauna represent 76 families.

How many endemics?

There is no clear consensus on how many bird species are endemic to Sri Lanka. The Ceylon Bird Club, the oldest ornithological organisation in the country, follows Priyantha Wijesinghe's checklist of 1994. This re-elevated Crimson-fronted Barbet, Black-throated Munia and Black-crested Bulbul to full species, endemic to Sri Lanka. Tim Inskipp *et al.* in the *Annotated Checklist of the Birds of the Oriental Region* and the Field Ornithology Group of Sri Lanka have followed Sibley and Monroe's list of 1990 and recognise 23 endemics. Many of the endemic subspecies are distinct in the field from related races on the mainland. As a result, further studies may conclude that the number of endemics is even higher than currently recognised. We have followed Wijesinghe's recognition of 26 endemics, which are listed below:

Sri Lanka Spurfowl *Galloperdix bicalcarata*
Sri Lanka Junglefowl *Gallus lafayettii*
Sri Lanka Wood Pigeon *Columba torringtonii*
Sri Lanka Hanging Parrot (Ceylon Lorikeet) *Loriculus beryllinus*
Layard's Parakeet *Psittacula calthropae*
Red-faced Malkoha *Phaenicophaeus pyrrhocephalus*
Green-billed Coucal *Centropus chlororhynchos*

Chestnut-backed Owlet *Glaucidium castanonotum*
Sri Lanka Grey Hornbill *Ocyceros gingalensis*
Yellow-fronted Barbet *Megalaima flavifrons*
Crimson-fronted Barbet (Ceylon Small Barbet) *Megalaima rubricapilla*
Black-crested Bulbul (Black-capped Bulbul) *Pycnonotus melanicterus*
Yellow-eared Bulbul *Pycnonotus penicillatus*
Sri Lanka Whistling Thrush *Myiophoneus blighi*
Spot-winged Thrush *Zoothera spiloptera*
Sri Lanka Bush Warbler (Ceylon Warbler) *Bradypterus palliseri*
Dull-blue Flycatcher (Dusky-blue Flycatcher) *Eumyias sordida*
Brown-capped Babbler *Pellorneum fuscocapillum*
Orange-billed Babbler (Ceylon Rufous Babbler) *Turdoides rufescens*
Ashy-headed Laughingthrush *Garrulax cinereifrons*
Legge's Flowerpecker *Dicaeum vincens*
Sri Lanka White-eye (Ceylon Hill White-eye) *Zosterops ceylonensis*
Sri Lanka Blue Magpie *Urocissa ornata*
White-faced Starling *Sturnus albofrontatus*
Sri Lanka Myna (Ceylon Hill-Myna) *Gracula ptilogenys*
Black-throated Munia (Ceylon Hill Munia) *Lonchura kelaarti*

Birds to look out for

For visiting birders, the birds of most interest will be the endemic species. For this reason, expanded accounts are provided in the text. In the case of a few highly sought after but 'difficult to see' birds such as the Sri Lanka Spurfowl, details on the best places to see them are given in the text. The sections on the endemics are heavily drawn from Deepal Warakagoda's Endemic Bird Finder in the Pica Traveller Sri Lanka. A carefully timed and planned itinerary with a local bird tour leader may succeed in seeing or hearing all of the endemics in as short a space of time as a week!

The island has a large number of endemic races (subspecies). Most are distinguished from the mainland forms by subtle differences in wing length etc. that are not apparent in the field. There are however a number of well-marked races that are of particular interest to the birder as there is potential for some of them to be elevated to full species status. The birder is advised to pay attention to the following distinct races.

Black-rumped Flameback (Red-backed Woodpecker) *Dinopium benghalense psarodes*
Greater Flameback (Crimson-backed Woodpecker) *Chrysocolaptes lucidus stricklandi*
Red-rumped Swallow (Ceylon Swallow) *Hirundo daurica hyperythra*
Scaly Thrush (Ceylon Scaly Thrush) *Zoothera dauma imbricata*
Blackbird *Turdus merula kinnisii*
Ashy Prinia *Prinia socialis brevicauda*
Jungle Prinia (Large Prinia) *Prinia sylvatica valida*
Indian Scimitar Babbler *Pomatorhinus horsfieldii melanurus*
Tawny-bellied Babbler *Dumetia hyperythra phillipsi*
Dark-fronted Babbler *Rhopocichla atriceps siccata*

Yellow-billed Babbler (Southern Common Babbler) *Turdoides affinis taprobanus*
Greater Racket-tailed Drongo (Ceylon Crested Drongo) *Dicrurus paradiseus lophorhinus*

Threatened Species

To highlight the perilous state of many of the resident birds, the threat category has been shown based on Thilo Hoffmann's *Threatened Birds of Sri Lanka: A National Red Data List* (1998). Hoffmann identified two threat categories. The category used in this book is what he considered as the threat category by the strict application of criteria laid by the International Union for the Conservation of Nature (IUCN). An empirical threat category employed by him often places the same bird in a less severe threat status. The threat category is in the context of a bird's distribution in Sri Lanka.

For a country with a reasonable number of amateur birdwatchers surprisingly few quantitative surveys have been undertaken. The lack of monitoring may mask the actual decline of many species.

What will you see?

The birds you see at a given place will be determined by the type of habitat or habitats the site has to offer. A national park like Ruhuna (Yala) and Bundala will often comprise a mixture of habitats comprising wetlands, lakes, dry scrub, grassland and rivers. A day's birding may yield over a hundred species. A rain forest like Sinharaja may throw up far fewer species, but they are likely to be more special. If you encounter a good mixed feeding flock, half a dozen endemics and a dozen other birds may be seen. To illustrate the diversity of bird life at different sites, actual examples of birds seen on field visits by the main author are reproduced below:

Uda Walawe National Park – dry zone scrub, grassland and lakes. The park is in the dry lowlands of Sri Lanka and comprises a varied mix of grassland, scrub jungle, tall forest and lakes. The list below is from a visit in April. A birdwatching trip could result in over a hundred species in a day, double the list below.

Spot-billed Pelican, Little Cormorant, Grey Heron, Indian Pond Heron, Cattle Egret, Large Egret, Little Egret, Intermediate Egret, Painted Stork, Woolly-necked Stork, Black-shouldered Kite, Brahminy Kite, White-bellied Sea Eagle, Grey-headed Fish Eagle, Serpent Eagle, Indian Peafowl, Red-wattled Lapwing, Yellow-wattled Lapwing, Little Ringed Plover, Wood Sandpiper, Black-winged Stilt, Whiskered Tern, Green Imperial Pigeon, Spotted Dove, Rose-ringed Parakeet, House Swift, Crested Treeswift, Common Kingfisher, Stork-billed Kingfisher, White-throated Kingfisher, Black-capped Kingfsher, Green Bee-eater, Indian Roller, Crimson-throated Barbet, Black-rumped Flameback, Rufous-winged Bush Lark, Barn Swallow, Brown Shrike, Black-headed Oriole, Common Myna, Large-billed Crow, Small Minivet, Red-vented Bulbul, Tawny-bellied Babbler, Yellow-eyed Babbler, White-browed Fantail, Asian

Paradise Flycatcher, Zitting Cisticola, Common Tailorbird, Magpie Robin, Indian Robin and Grey-headed Yellow Wagtail.

Talangama Lake – wet zone, suburban wetland
Talangama Lake is a beautiful site on the outskirts of Colombo with great potential as an urban nature reserve. The list below is based on a late morning visit in December.

Lesser Whistling-duck, Asian Paradise Flycatcher, Oriental White-eye, Brown-capped Pygmy Woodpecker, Black-rumped Flameback, Asian Palm Swift, Little Egret, Intermediate Egret, Great Egret, Cattle Egret, Yellow Bittern, Indian Cormorant, Little Cormorant, Common Sandpiper, Wood Sandpiper, Little Grebe, Pintail Snipe, Black-winged Stilt, Black-headed Ibis, Barn Swallow, Rose-ringed Parakeet, Indian Pond Heron, White-breasted Waterhen, Purple Heron, Common Kingfisher, Blue-tailed Bee-eater , White-browed Bulbul, Ashy Woodswallow, Red-wattled Lapwing and Brahminy Kite.

Morapitiya – lowland rain forest
Morapitiya is a tract of rain forest that adjoins the better known Sinharaja Man and Biosphere Reserve. To illustrate the impact that habitat has on species, the actual sequence in which the species were encountered is given with an indication of the habitat. However, a number of species will occur in a range of habitats and it is only a select few such as Ashy-headed Laughingthrush which are confined to good rain forest. The visit was in January when forest migrants such as Brown-breasted Flycatcher were present.

Degraded habitat comprising a mixture of mature Jak trees, tea, abandoned paddy, rubber with pockets of secondary forest.

Black Bulbul, White-bellied Drongo, Southern Hill Myna, Purple-rumped Sunbird, Crimson-fronted Barbet, Yellow-fronted Barbet, Green Imperial Pigeon, White-breasted Waterhen, Sri Lanka Hanging Parrot, White-throated Kingfisher, Common Tailorbird, Asian Koel, Brown-headed Barbet, Greater Coucal, Black-headed Oriole, Asian Paradise Flycatcher, Brown Flycatcher, Yellow-browed Bulbul, Spotted Dove, Yellow-billed Babbler, Black-rumped Flameback, Oriental Magpie Robin, Red-vented Bulbul, Common Myna, Grey Hornbill, Pale-billed Flowerpecker, Indian Pond Heron, Brown-capped Babbler, Black-crested Bulbul, Red-rumped Swallow, Brown Shrike, Iora, Emerald Dove and Indian Swiftlet.

Good secondary forest
Bar-winged Flycatcher-shrike, Dark-fronted Babbler, Malabar Trogon, Green-billed Coucal , Ceylon Crested Drongo (Greater Racket-tailed Drongo), Sri Lanka Blue Magpie, Sri Lanka Spurfowl (heard), Scarlet Minivet, Crested Serpent Eagle, Brown-breasted Flycatcher, Ashy-headed Laughingthrush, Orange-billed Babbler and Indian Scimitar Babbler.

Information for visitors

Preparation
Some preparation can make a lot of difference in a small accessible island like Sri Lanka. A good deal of information is available both on the internet as well as from traditional bookshops.

Internet
For information on any recent trip reports, the internet flyway in the Oriental Bird Club's web page (http://www.orientalbirdclub. org/) is a good place to start a search. E-mail discussion forums like UK Bird Net and the NatHistory South India are also good places from which to solicit information. Details on signing up for these free e-mail discussion groups are on the OBC web site.

Books
For pre-trip reading and use in the field the *Pica Traveller Sri Lanka*, lead authored by Gehan de Silva Wijeyeratne, is invaluable. It is the most comprehensive travel guide for birdwatchers, wildlife and cultural enthusiasts and activity holiday seekers. It has accounts on the fauna and flora, checklists, detailed descriptions of wildlife and cultural sites and over a hundred maps. A pocket photographic guide such as this is adequate for most birds that a visitor on a short trip, or a resident with a casual interest is likely to see. Keen birdwatchers should consider a fully fledged field guide although these are heavier and more expensive. The best is *A Field Guide to the Birds of Sri Lanka* by John Harrison and Tim Worfolk. The plates show different plumages, sexes, colour morphs, races etc. making it invaluable for birders. GM Henry's *Guide to the Birds of Sri Lanka* complements the Harrison field guide.

Sound recordings
Keen birdwatchers should consider familiarising themselves with the calls and songs of Sri Lankan birds. A comprehensive compilation on three tapes has been issued by local wildlife sound recordist Deepal Warakagoda, the co-author of this book. This is the benchmark sound recording set.

Wildlife art
The lead authors run an art gallery in Colombo at 155 Model Farm Road, by appointment only, selling paintings, prints and recordings. Phone Deepal on 01 810604 or Gehan or Nirma on 01 672230.

Organised tours
A number of birding tours operate to Sri Lanka. These may not always be convenient for a family with young children or for those for whom birding may not be the only priority. A number of local tour companies will organise a package involving birdwatching, culture and even chilling out on the beach, all tailored to individual request. Some of the better known companies, all in Colombo, are listed below. The international phone code for Colombo is + 94 +1.

A Baur & Co. (Travels), Baurs Building, 5 Upper Chatham Street, Colombo 1. Tel: 448087, 448822, 320551-6. Fax: 448493. E-mail: tourism@baurs.com. Website: www.baurs.com

Aitken Spence Travels, 305 Vauxhall Street, Colombo 3. Tel: 345112 to 23. Fax: 436382

Hemtours, 6th Floor, Hemas House, 75 Braybrooke Place, Colombo 2. Tel: 300001/2. Fax: 300003/4. E-mail: hemtours@sri.lanka.net

Lanka Sportreizen, 211, Hospital Road, Kalubowila, Dehiwala. Tel: 824500, 824955, 828251. Fax: 826125. E-mail: lsr@sri.lanka.net. Contact D. K. R. Dharmapala or Thilak Weerasinghe.

Jetwing Eco Holidays, Specialists in Birding, Rainforest & Wildlife Tours, Jetwing House, 46/26 Nawam Mawatha, Colombo 02, Sri Lanka. Tel: ++94-1-345700 or ++94-1-381201. Fax: ++94-1-441289. E-mail: eco@jetwing.lk. Website: www.jetwingeco.com Contact Gehan de Silva Wijeyeratne.

Quickshaws Tours, 3 Kalinga Place, off Jawatte Road, Colombo 5. Their correspondence address is P. O. Box 1830, Colombo. Tel: 583133/5, 582995. Fax: 587613. E-mail: quiktur@lankacom.net.

Twitter Holidays, Delmege Forsyth Tours, 101 Vinayalankara Mawatha, Colombo 10. Tel: 693361, 693367, 686151, 699984, 699500. Fax: 698139, 699413, 686149. E-mail: delmege@sri.lanka.net

Walker Tours, 130 Glennie Street, Colombo 2. Tel: 421101 to 8, 439053. Fax: 447087, 493026. Website: www.keels.com/walkers. E-mail: dreamhol@walkers.slt.lk

When to go

The period November to April is best for visiting birders. February and March are the best months: there are two reasons for this. Firstly you will avoid the monsoons. Secondly the migrants are still present. Indian Pitta and Pied Thrush, the two favourites amongst birders, are still around. Waders will also be moulting into breeding plumage offering the opportunity to study this difficult group in different plumages. August and September are two other relatively dry months in which migrants also occur.

The best birding sites

If you are after the endemics make it a point to visit a lowland rain forest like Kitulgala or Sinharaja. 17 of the 26 endemics have been recorded in Sinharaja. However, certain montane species like Yellow-eared Bulbul are usually seen only on its eastern borders which are generally not visited by birdwatchers. To see the montane specialities, it is necessary to visit a site such as Hakgala or Horton Plains. Endemics such as Dull-blue Flycatcher, Sri Lanka

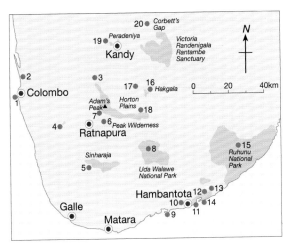

Key

1. Bellanwila Attidiya Sanctuary
2. Muthurajawela Marshes
3. Kitulgala or Kelani Valley Forest Reserve
4. Bodhinagala or Ingiriya Forest Reserve
5. Sinharaja Man and Biosphere Reserve
6. Gilimale Forest Reserve
7. Adam's Peak Trail: Carney Estate
8. Uda Walawe National Park
9. Kalametiya Sanctuary
10. Karagan Lewaya
11. Hambantota Maha Lewaya
12. Embilikala Kalapuwa
13. Bundala Lewaya
14. Bundala National Park
15. Ruhunu National Park (Yala West)
16. Hakgala
17. Victoria Park
18. Horton Plains National Park
19. Udawattakele Sanctuary
20. Knuckles Range: Corbett's Gap

Whistling Thrush and Sri Lanka Bush Warbler occur here. These two sites are also good places for endemics like Sri Lanka Wood Pigeon which may be seen in lower elevations during seasonal movements. If you only have time to visit two places, Sinharaja and Horton Plains provide the top choices for birders.

The best chance of seeing the endemic Green-billed Coucal was previously at Bodhinagala. However, recent forest clearance has made it difficult to see this species, but this site produces other good forest birds. For mammal enthusiasts, the national parks of Bundala, Yala and Uda Walawe are recommended. Uda Walawe is particularly good for elephants and birds of prey. The family with no time for specialist birding can still see over 100 species even if they are on the cultural triangle circuit. The north central plains are replete with ancient reservoirs. These are known locally as tanks or 'wewas'. These are a haven for wildlife in much the same way as flooded gravel pits are in Europe. For more information obtain a copy of the *Pica Traveller Sri Lanka* which has extensive details of sites for the casual birdwatcher as well as the specialist birder.

Key to corner tabs

 Grebes & cormorants

 Herons, storks & allies

 Ducks

 Raptors

 Gamebirds

 Rails & allies

 Waders

 Gulls & terns

 Pigeons & doves

 Parrots & parakeets

 Cuckoos & relatives

 Nightbirds

 Swifts & swallows

 Kingfishers

 Bee-eaters, rollers & hoopoes

 Hornbills

 Barbets & woodpeckers

 Pittas

 Larks, pipits & wagtails

 Cuckoo-shrikes, minivets & leafbirds

 Bulbuls

 Thrushes & robins

 Warblers

 Flycatchers

 Babblers

 Tits & nuthatches

 Sunbirds

 Flowerpeckers

 White-eyes

 Shrikes

 Drongos

 Magpies & crows

 Starlings & mynas

 Sparrows, weavers & munias

The species descriptions

The species accounts are necessarily brief and have been written to convey where possible the general impression or 'character portrait' of a bird. This is complemented by a discussion of its distinct features, either in terms of its plumage or its habits. Descriptive information on plumage has been kept to a bare minimum where this is amply conveyed by the photographs. In species in which the sexes are different, both sexes have been described. Where a species is likely to be confused with another, the information on identification has been suitably expanded. Endemics are marked with a *.

Details of distribution are given for the species and vocalisations are described mostly with transcriptions where such information is helpful or aids identification. However, transcribing a bird's call to reflect the true character of its sound is difficult, and the transcription may vary from person to person. Therefore, there is no substitute to learning the calls in the field or from commercially available tapes of bird sounds. The various aspects of a species account is not presented in a regimented order but are written to 'go with the flow' of each account of a species. Some of the pelagic species like Shearwaters, Petrels etc. have been excluded from the book as they are unlikely to be seen, unless on a special sea-cruise for seabirds.

In this book we follow the standard sequence of Orders and Families by Voous in the *Dictionary of Birds* (1985) by David Lack. The recent sequence proposed by Sibley and Monroe based on DNA-DNA hybridization studies is radically different from this. The names given mostly follow those in the OBC Checklist. English names used locally are also given where they are significantly different.

Bird topography

The illustration below shows the main parts of a bird used in descriptions of plumage and anatomy. A knowledge of these terms will be useful for identification purposes.

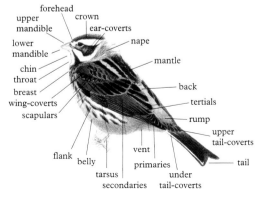

T.S.U. de Zylva

A small, duck-like bird of tanks, lakes and marshes. Unlike the ducks, it has a pointed beak and lacks a tail. Usually occurs in pairs, but at times flocks to form rafts of birds. Dives regularly when feeding. The birds prefer to stay close to a reed-fringed shoreline. In non-breeding plumage, the birds are nondescript dull brown with a dark cap. In breeding plumage, the face and neck become a deep chestnut and a pale patch develops around the gape of the bill. Courting male's song is a long-drawn, trilling whinny. A fairly common resident in suitable lowland habitats and sometimes occurs at higher altitudes.

Red-billed Tropicbird *Phaethon aethereus* 48 cm
(plus 50 cm tail)

Ismeth Raheem

Tropicbirds are scarce, sought after birds. Resembles a large tern, but has a heavy bill and elongated central tail feathers. Has fine wavy bars on upperparts, a red bill, distinct black eye stripe, and unmarked head, neck and underparts. Black outer primaries and primary coverts form a broad black band along edge of fore-wing after carpal joint. Immatures have yellow to orange bill and lack elongated central tail feathers. A scarce but regular migrant to the south-western coast, mainly during February to August. Birds feed at sea in the morning but come to shore in the afternoon to roost on coconut palms. Utters a harsh *kraak* call in flight at times.

Little Cormorant *Phalacrocorax niger* 51 cm

Common throughout, in smaller numbers in the hills. Differs from Great Cormorant (*Phalacrocorax carbo*) in its smaller size and rather rounded head with shorter beak. Juvenile brownish. Non-breeding adult and juvenile have some white and yellow on the face, but differs from contrasting facial pattern of Great Cormorant. Breeding adult has small crest on forehead and a few white filaments on the face. Indian Cormorant (*Phalacrocorax fuscicollis*), with which Little Cormorant often associates, is bigger and heavier-looking. Little Cormorant also has relatively shorter and more conically-shaped bill. Unlike them, seen on rivers in wet zone forest. Seen in hundreds on large water bodies that dot the dry zone. Generally silent, although at roosts some unmusical croaks may be uttered.

T.S.U. de Zylva

Indian Cormorant (Indian Shag)
Phalacrocorax fuscicollis 64 cm

T.S.U. de Zylva

Common and widespread waterbird that ascends to the lower hills. Often associates with Little Cormorant (*Phalacrocorax niger*). Indian Cormorant seems to prefer large open bodies of water; large flocks occur in dry zone. Less frequent on small rivers than Little Cormorant. Distinguished from Little Cormorant by its larger size, heavier build and conspicuous scaly effect on the plumage. The beak is longish and thin, unlike in Little Cormorant. Its irides are emerald green, but this is only conspicuous at close range.

15

Great Cormorant *Phalacrocorax carbo* 80–100 cm

Ravi Samarasinha

(Vulnerable). The largest cormorant in the island. Similar to Indian Cormorant (*Phalacrocorax fuscicollis*) but difference in size very apparent when both are together, and the beak of the latter is much more slender. White on throat distinctive and very prominent with a bright yellow patch at bill base during breeding season. Variable white on head and neck, and white patch on the flanks. Juvenile has browner upperparts and white underparts. A rather rare resident in the dry lowlands; birds often occur with the other two cormorant species. Will congregate at large tanks, especially during the breeding season.

Darter (Indian Darter) *Anhinga melanogaster* 85–97 cm

T.S.U. de Zylva

A relatively uncommon resident waterbird in the dry lowlands. Occasionally found in the wet lowlands. The long, snake-like neck and long pointed beak easily distinguish it from the cormorants. In breeding plumage, the black upperparts are streaked strongly with silvery filaments. In the water, it submerges itself except for the long neck and beak earning itself the name of 'snake bird'. The degree of submergence is greater than that of the cormorants, making their profiles in the water very different. Often associates with flocks of cormorants, but solitary birds are not uncommon.

Spot-billed Pelican *Pelecanus philippensis* 127–140 cm

T.S.U. de Zylva

(Vulnerable). An internationally endangered species found in good numbers in tanks and lagoons of dry lowlands. Forms flocks, and is one of the largest waterbirds on the island. There are two rows of dark spots on its long, flat upper mandible and a large pouch hangs beneath lower mandible. This pouch is enlarged when the pelican is feeding. Breeding plumage whiter than non-breeding plumage, and greyish-pink on the lower back, rump, flanks and undertail-coverts. The pouch and the bare skin around the eye become brighter. Juvenile has brown upperparts and pale bare parts. Dehiwela Zoo in Colombo has a good, free-ranging, nesting population which spreads out to wet zone lakes.

Yellow Bittern *Ixobrychus sinensis* 36–38 cm

T.S.U. de Zylva

Fairly common waterbird throughout lowlands and will ascend to mid hills. Common in reedbeds but tends to skulk in thick vegetation. The smallest bittern found in Sri Lanka. Easily separated from Cinnamon Bittern (*Ixobrychus cinnamomeus*) by black flight feathers which contrast with buff-yellow fore-wing. It also has a black tail. Male has black cap and more uniformly coloured body. Female has no black on head with overall darker plumage and few long brown lines along sides of the neck. Juvenile closely resembles female but has pale spots on wings. Gives strong, rather harsh sounding call *kek* or *ke-e-e-k*, sometimes repeated. Resident breeding population small; the majority of birds are migrants.

17

Cinnamon Bittern (Chestnut Bittern)
Ixobrychus cinnamomeus 38–41 cm

(Vulnerable). Uncommon, occurring throughout lowlands and sometimes to the higher hills. Found in reed-fringed, tangled vegetation. Easily overlooked unless one flies from one clump of vegetation to another. Uniform chestnut upperparts, and noticeably larger than Yellow Bittern (*Ixobrychus sinensis*). Non-contrasting cinnamon upperparts distinguish it from heavily contrasting Yellow Bittern. Female browner and has mottling on the wings and yellow lores. Male has red lores. Juvenile mottled brown with conspicuous, chestnut-coloured wings which show well in flight. Birds will 'freeze' to avoid detection. Utters a croaking flight-call, and male gives a rapid, low-pitched six or seven syllable song *hohohohohohoho*, often repeated during breeding season.

Black Bittern *Dupetor flavicollis* 54–61 cm

Unmistakable with overall black upperparts, yellow neck stripe and yellow streaking on fore-neck. Fairly common in lowlands during migrant season, especially in wet zone where it may ascend to the mid hills. Like other bitterns, found in typical marshy habitats. However, Black Bittern may also be found quietly stalking along a forested stream. The numbers of birds can vary greatly due to the relatively small local populations being augmented by wintering birds. Female browner on upperparts and juvenile dull with mottled brown upperparts. Sometimes utters a croaking call *ak, ak, ak* in flight.

18

Malayan Night Heron (Malay Bittern)
Gorsachius melanolophus 48–51 cm

T.S.U. de Zylva

A scarce but regular migrant. Differs from the other bitterns in that it may be encountered anywhere on the island in suitable forested streams rather than in open wetlands. Adult chestnut with a black crown and nuchal crest. Juvenile dark with fine whitish barring and dark crest with white tips. Very secretive and keeps to thick cover, stealthily clambering about on vegetation. It is mainly active after dusk and is seldom seen in daylight, which is one reason why it is rarely reported.

Black-crowned Night Heron *Nycticorax nycticorax* 58–65 cm

T.S.U. de Zylva

Fairly common resident in the lowlands up to the lower hills. The black, grey and whitish plumage, and red eye make adult unmistakeable. A few long white plumes develop on the nape of breeding adults and the legs turn reddish for a few days. Juvenile brown, with a streaked head and breast, and with heavy white spotting to upperparts, very different in pattern to any of the bitterns. Despite its name, it can be active by day. As dusk falls, these birds leave their roost, drawing attention to themselves as they fly to the nearest hunting ground uttering harsh *kwaak* flight calls.

19

Little Heron (Little Green Heron) *Butorides striatus* 40–48 cm

T.S.U. de Zylva

An uncommon, widespread small heron, in the lowlands and lower hills. Most likely to be seen in mangrove habitats on the coast. Its preference for mangroves or vegetation-fringed rivers and its small size result in it being less commonly seen than the larger herons of open marshes. Typically seen as lone individuals, with more careful searching along the water's edge revealing more birds. Greyish-green overall, with a dark cap. In flight, it looks dark on the upper wing as the darker flight feathers contrast little. An alarm-call uttered in flight is *kyek, kyek*.

Indian Pond Heron *Ardeola grayii* 42–45 cm

T.S.U. de Zylva

Common throughout the country, although more abundant in lowlands. Found wherever there are wet areas and will readily take to water-logged cricket fields. Cryptically camouflaged, exploding into a white flash as it takes wing. The white of its wings is concealed at rest by its mantle and scapular feathers that give it a streaked, mud brown look. Breeding plumage mainly soft greyish-buff, with maroon mantle and blue facial skin, and a few long white plumes on the nape. During its brief, peak breeding condition, its legs turn red. Vagrant Chinese Pond Heron (*Ardeola bacchus*) is virtually indistinguishable in non-breeding plumage. Sometimes utters a croaking call.

Cattle Egret *Bubulcus ibis* 48–53 cm

The smallest of the egrets. Differs from other egrets by its stocky build, roundish head, shorter and broader-based yellow beak, and a prominent chin. In breeding season, beak becomes brighter, and head, neck and mantle turn golden-buff, unlike in other egrets. Very common resident of open fields; flocks also gather at large garbage dumps. Small flocks often associate with water buffaloes. It feeds on insects disturbed by the buffaloes, and will also ride on their backs to pick off ticks and lice. Distributed throughout the island up to the higher hills, but commonest in the lowlands.

T.S.U. de Zylva

Western Reef Egret (Indian Reef Heron)
Egretta gularis 55–65 cm

(Vulnerable). Fairly rare winter migrant to coasts. Similar in shape and size to Little Egret (*Egretta garzetta*) but has thicker bill. Bill usually brownish with yellowish base or entirely yellowish, and yellow or greenish on feet extends up to about hock-joint, unlike in Little Egret. Reef Egret occurs in two colour-morphs: dark morph has dark ashy-grey body with white chin and throat, whereas pale morph has either pure white plumage or white plumage with grey patches. All-white birds can be confused with

T.S.U. de Zylva

Little Egret but can be separated by shape and colour of bill, and colour of legs. A coastal species found on reefs, on the coast or by lagoons. In the 19th century, the bird was a breeding resident.

21

Little Egret *Egretta garzetta* 55–65 cm

The pencil-thin black beak and graceful build distinguish this species from other egrets even if the yellow feet cannot be seen. The Sri Lankan race always has yellow feet and black legs, unlike other races found in mainland Asia. Common throughout the lowlands and the hills; found in canals, lakes, ponds and wet fields. This is the egret most likely to be seen on waterways and ditches in built-up areas. In the breeding season, it develops nuptial plumes on head, breast and back. Its diet is mainly fish and other aquatic animals. It often mixes with flocks of other egrets when feeding and breeding.

T.S.U. de Zylva

Intermediate Egret *Mesophoyx intermedia* 65–72 cm

T.S.U. de Zylva

Common resident found throughout lowlands up to the higher hills. Non-breeding Intermediate Egret looks similar to non-breeding Cattle Egret (*Bubulcus ibis*), with black legs and yellow bill. However, Intermediate is larger, and has a longer bill and neck, with an obvious 'S' shape and prominent kink on fore-neck (see also Cattle Egret). Distinguished from Little Egret (*Egretta garzetta*) by larger size and heavier bill, which is yellow on non-breeding bird. In breeding plumage, bill black (often with a yellow base) and plumes develop only on breast and back. Smaller than Great Egret (*Casmerodius albus*), neck kink closer to head.

Great Egret *Casmerodius albus* 85–102 cm

The largest egret, common in lowlands and up to mid hills. Commonest in dry zone on weed-fringed man-made reservoirs. Distinguished from other egrets by large size, and long neck with a prominent kink on fore-neck, which makes for a larger curve in the upper-neck than that in Intermediate Egret (*Mesophoyx intermedia*). Its gape line, at base of the bill, extends behind and below eye. In breeding plumage, strong yellow beak with a dusky tip turns all-black, tibia which are normally dusky yellow turn crimson. Plumes develop only on back. Often seen as lone individuals, although congregations do occur with other egrets, in paddy fields which are being ploughed.

T.S.U. de Zylva

Grey Heron *Ardea cinerea* 90–98 cm

A large long-necked heron, fairly common at the water's edge in the dry lowlands. Rare in the wet zone where Purple Heron (*Ardea purpurea*) seems to be the commoner species. The overall grey colour with two black broken lines on the white neck and breast, black markings on crown and black patch on either side of breast are distinctive. The yellow beak develops a crimson flush and yellow legs become crimson during the peak of the breeding season. Juvenile uniform grey without black markings and crest. Utters a loud *kaack* usually repeated on the wing as a contact call. Its diet is mainly fish and other aquatic animals such as frogs.

T.S.U. de Zylva

Purple Heron *Ardea purpurea* 78–90 cm

A large dark long-necked heron which is a fairly common in the wetlands of the low country. It is rather less common in the dry zone. Despite its size, and reddish and dark grey colour, it blends well with the aquatic vegetation. It stalks through the aquatic vegetation for frogs, fish and other aquatic animals. It contorts its head into odd angles and freezes in that position, striking swiftly to capture its prey. Leisurely flapping flight with trailing legs. Juvenile overall uniform brown. Utters loud series of harsh croaks especially when disturbed.

Painted Stork *Mycteria leucocephala* 93–102 cm

Found in good numbers in water bodies within the larger protected areas in dry lowlands. The birds seen in the wet zone around Colombo are from colony in Dehiwela Zoo. At times, large flocks may be seen soaring on thermals. The orange facial skin and slightly down-curved yellow beak readily identify this species. In flight, underwing shows little contrast as underwing-coverts are longitudinally barred black and white. Its belly pattern is also different to any other Sri Lankan stork, having white underparts with a broad breast band formed by fine black barring. Juvenile mainly grey and brown. Sifts through mud and water for aquatic prey.

24

Asian Openbill (Openbill) *Anastomus oscitans* 68–81 cm

Commonest widespread stork throughout the lowlands. Found in marshes, tanks or even paddy fields. The gap in the mandibles giving rise to its name is not particularly obvious with the naked eye unless seen side-on. Almost always found in small flocks. Adult with black and pure white breeding plumage reminiscent of White Stork (*Ciconia ciconia*), a vagrant to Sri Lanka. The underwing pattern is identical to White Stork. However, Openbill's black, not white, tail and unusual brownish-black bill will separate it from White Stork which has red bill. Juvenile grey with hint of brown. Non-breeding adult greyish.

T.S.U. de Zylva

Woolly-necked Stork (White-necked Stork)
Ciconia episcopus 75–92 cm

Small stork with unmistakable plumage pattern. Uncommon resident in dry lowlands. Seems to be confined to areas where human population density is low. Remote areas in the north-central province and the national parks seem to offer the best chance of seeing this bird. Usually in pairs, but uncommonly in small flocks. Tends to perch on trees at rest, unlike Painted Stork (*Mycteria leucocephala*) which squats on ground. Confusion unlikely with vagrant Black Stork (*Ciconia nigra*), which is similar size but has black neck and red bill. From below, Woolly-necked Stork has dark wings and a broad black band across the breast on white underparts.

T.S.U. de Zylva

25

Black-necked Stork *Ephippiorhynchus asiaticus* 121–135 cm

(Critically endangered). The tallest bird in the island. Nationally endangered bird with at most a handful of breeding pairs in the south of the country. The only reliable place to see it is Ruhunu National Park. Despite its rarity, many people do manage to see it as it likes to feed in open water or at marshy edges of lakes. The black beak and neck, and height of this bird render it conspicuous. Male has dark brown iris; female yellow. Otherwise sexes similar. In flight, underwing pattern distinctive with a broad black band running through the middle of otherwise white underwing.

T.S.U. de Zylva

Lesser Adjutant *Leptoptilos javanicus* 115–125 cm

(Endangered). This bulky stork is the largest bird on the island. Rather rare resident in wetlands of forested areas in dry lowlands. Looking rather ungainly and grotesque with its bare face, Lesser Adjutant is unlikely to be confused with any other stork. Single birds often occur far from water in scrub jungle. One or two birds typically seen at a waterhole although exceptionally a dozen or more may occur together during dry season. The only stork which flies with its neck retracted into the shoulders. From below, dark wings contrast with white underparts, and it has broader wings than the other storks. In breeding plumage, beak develops a reddish tinge, bare brown face becomes more red, and bare neck becomes bright yellow.

T.S.U. de Zylva

Glossy Ibis *Plegadis falcinellus* 55–65 cm

T.S.U. de Zylva

Formerly a breeding resident in the low country, but became extinct in the island towards the end of the 19th century. Records of it in the mid 20th century created a lot of interest, and by the end of the 20th century it had become established as a scarce but regular migrant. Flocks of a dozen or more birds are seen at the Bellanwila Attidiya Sanctuary with records from the larger wetlands in the south and north-central province. Identified by typical ibis shape, in particular decurved bill and overall dark plumage. Smaller than common Black-headed Ibis (*Threskiornis melanocephalus*).

Black-headed Ibis (White Ibis)
Threskiornis melanocephalus 75 cm

Found throughout the lowlands wherever suitable habitat occurs. Prefers lake fringes with stretches of undisturbed habitat, hence tends to be seen in good-sized flocks, mainly in the dry zone. The black and white plumage, distinctive decurved black bill and naked black head make confusion impossible. In its breeding plumage, develops white plumes on breast and grey plumes on back. Juvenile has grey feathers on neck. Flocks are often seen in the mornings and evenings in V-shaped formations flying to and from roosts. Most 'tanks' in the dry zone support this species.

T.S.U. de Zylva

27

Eurasian Spoonbill *Platalea leucorodia* 82–90 cm

T.S.U. de Zylva

Resident occurring in low numbers but quite likely to be seen in the national parks on the southern coastal belt. The black bill ends in a spoon shape that has a yellow patch. In breeding plumage it develops a crest of longish white feathers on nape and yellow colour on breast. Juvenile lacks yellow patch at bill tip. Spoonbills are usually seen standing together in small flocks. In flight, at first glance similar to Black-headed Ibis (*Threskiornis melanocephalus*), but have white and not black necks.

Greater Flamingo *Phoenicopterus ruber* 125–145 cm

T.S.U. de Zylva

A large, whitish, stork-like bird with short beak of unusual shape, making it impossible to confuse with any other bird. Its breeding habits remain a mystery. Birds found in Sri Lanka are believed to breed in the Rann of Kutch, India. However, present throughout the year. In any flock, birds vary in size due to age and sex, potentially leading to confusion with smaller Lesser Flamingo (*Phoenicopterus minor*), although the latter has never been authentically recorded. Immature smaller and greyer with dark bill. Non-breeding adult and older immature have grey base to bill. Breeding adult develops pinkish wash to plumage and pink bill base. Flocks utter a honking *ak, ak*. Most likely seen in salt pans of south around Hambantota and Bundala.

28

Lesser Whistling-duck (Lesser Whistling Teal)
Dendrocygna javanica 38–42 cm

T.S.U. de Zylva

A small, brown duck, common in well-vegetated shallow lakes. Found throughout the island to the lower hills. Small flocks fly to and from roosts uttering whistling calls that give the species its name. Small flocks of this bird manage to survive wherever there are wetlands, despite years of persecution by hunters. Vagrant Fulvous Whistling-duck (*Dendrocygna bicolor*) is larger and has conspicuous white streaks on the flanks. It also has uniformly dark wings unlike Lesser which has maroon coverts that contrast with dark wings.

Cotton Pygmy-goose (Cotton Teal)
Nettapus coromandelianus 33–38 cm

T.S.U. de Zylva

The smallest resident duck. A dainty and easily overlooked bird of open lakes, it occurs throughout the low country. Although not abundant, small flocks can be found on marsh-fringed lakes. Relatively shy, preferring to keep away from people. Breeding male has glossy blackish-green back and collar, a broad white band across the wing in flight, and grey and white underparts. Female has dull-black back, drab underparts and a dark eye-line. Non-breeding male resembles female, with- (Top) *male;* (above) *female*

out the dark collar but with an eye-line and white wingbar. Flight rapid, often skimming the surface. In courtship several males fly behind a female uttering their honking calls.

29

Northern Pintail *Anas acuta* 51–66 cm

T.S.U. de Zylva

Fairly common migrant to the lowlands of the dry zone, sometimes seen in large flocks especially in the coastal wetlands. Occasionally found in the wet zone. Male easily recognised by chocolate brown head and white stripe tapering up each side of the neck, and the long thin 'pintail'. Female brown overall with dark markings and longish pointed tail; can be confused with females of other large ducks but colour of beak, legs and speculum in flight separate it. Non-breeding male resembles female. The lead grey colour of the beak is useful for separating females and eclipse males from females of other ducks.

Garganey *Anas querquedula* 36–41 cm

T.S.U. de Zylva

Unmistakable small duck. Breeding male has attractive plumage with a conspicuous broad white eyebrow. It has a brown head, neck and breast, grey back and light grey underparts. Female brown with dark markings and faint pale eyebrow. Male in eclipse plumage and female may be confused with female Common Teal (*Anas crecca*). However, the latter has less obvious face markings and lacks white throat. In flight, shows a green speculum with a white leading edge to it. An abundant winter visitor to the dry-zone lowlands with the greatest concentrations on the larger lakes and lagoons. Small flocks are found throughout the wet lowlands.

Northern Shoveler (Shoveler) *Anas clypeata* 43–52 cm

T.S.U. de Zylva

The long spatulate bill makes this species impossible to confuse
with any other duck. In non-breeding plumage sexes are similar.
Breeding male is distinctive with green head, white breast and
chestnut on the belly and sides. In flight, both sexes have a blue-
grey upper fore-wing. Male has green speculum with a white
leading edge to it. Female speculum is dark but retains white
leading edge. Both sexes have underwing-coverts white. An
uncommon migrant encountered mainly in the *wewas* of the dry
lowlands. Feeding birds may form 'rotating circles'.

Tufted Duck *Aythya fuligula* 40–47 cm

Gehan de Silva Wijeyeratne

Rare vagrant to the lakes of the dry lowlands. The black and white
male in breeding plumage with its golden eye is unmistakable. Beak
is blue-grey with a black tip. Breeding male also has black nuchal
crest. Female and eclipse male brown overall and retain golden eye.
A stocky duck which prefers open water. In water, the body is little
submerged, when not diving. In flight both sexes show clear white
wingbar. It has a pugnacious air to it. Some females show a 'scaup'
face, with white on the face around the bill.

Oriental Honey-Buzzard
Pernis ptilorhynchus 55–65 cm

Gehan De Silva Wijeyeratne

Fairly common medium-large raptor found throughout the island. The resident population is augmented by the arrival of honey-buzzards from India during migration. Usually seen soaring. Small head and thin, longish neck in comparison to larger body is characteristic, and helps to identify honey-buzzard from other raptors. Adults darker brown above with variable underparts, from dark brown to light brown, or dark streaks or bars on paler background. Immature lighter having pale brown upperparts with whitish upperwing-coverts and almost whitish underparts. Call is a loud, rather drawn out *keeak*, which is seldom uttered. Male has grey face and red irides.

Black-winged Kite *Elanus caeruleus* 31–35 cm

T.S.U. de Zylva

Small, elegant raptor found throughout the island but more frequent in the open dry lowlands, and in hills over open grassy slopes. Uncommon resident, it may be seen perched solitarily on dead trees and sometimes on tall posts or wires. The red eye and black shoulders on grey and white plumage make it a distinctive bird. Hovers while hunting for prey, dropping on it with characteristic raised wings. In flight underwing shows a dark tip contrasting with pale underparts. It glides distinctively with the wings held at an angle. Sexes similar. Juvenile more grey-brown above, with rusty streaking on the breast.

32

Brahminy Kite *Haliastur indus* 44–52 cm

Widely distributed from lowlands to high elevations. Often seen fishing on open lakes, tanks, at sea and sometimes along rivers. Common raptor at Beira Lake and Colombo harbour. At times, 30 or more birds can be seen together. Adult has distinctive white head and breast, and chestnut-brown body. Juvenile overall brown and can be confused with other medium-sized raptors with similar plumage such as buzzards, harriers or Black Kite (*Milvus migrans*). Juvenile and adult have an almost unmarked shorter and more rounded tail than other similar-looking raptors. Juvenile has larger greyish-brown patch on dark underwing. A rather loud mewing call *aaeh* is uttered infrequently.

T.S.U. de Zylva

White-bellied Sea Eagle *Haliaeetus leucogaster* 66–71 cm

T.S.U. de Zylva

T.S.U. de Zylva

(Above) *adult;* (right) *sub-adult*

A large grey and white eagle which frequents wet habitats. In flight dark flight feathers contrast with white underwing-coverts, and has characteristic white tail which is short and wedge-shaped, with black band to base. Young birds overall brown; body whitens with maturity. In flight shows large pale patch at base of dark primaries on underwing, and whitish tail with black terminal band. Utters series of loud honking calls *ank, ank* during breeding. Rather uncommon resident found along coast and inland waters in the dry lowlands, and also in the Kandy area in the lower hills. A visitor to wet lowlands and higher hills, occasionally even seen over Colombo. Adults are unlikely to be confused with any other raptor.

33

Grey-headed Fish-eagle *Icthyophaga icthyaetus* 69–74 cm

Gehan De Silva Wijeyeratne

(Vulnerable). This magnificent raptor is restricted mainly to the 'tanks' (man-made lakes) of the low country dry zone. Has grey head, overall brownish plumage with contrasting white belly and undertail-coverts, and white tail with black terminal band. Young White-bellied Sea Eagles (*Haliaeetus leucogaster*) which occur in same habitats have superficial resemblance, especially to immatures, of this eagle. At all ages, fish eagles have white on belly, a whitish tail with black terminal band, which protrudes beyond tips of closed wings, and a somewhat smaller head with thinner neck, which gives a rather vulturine appearance. Its underwings are all black. It utters a loud unmusical honking *ohh, oooh*.

Crested Serpent-eagle *Spilornis cheela spilogaster* 56–74 cm

T.S.U. de Zylva

The most widespread and common larger raptor, from lowland and hilly forest to open areas. The crest is only evident when raised in excitement. Often soars in circles uttering a plaintive, screaming whistle *queeeu, quiu, quiu*. The underwing has a distinct banding, with dark trailing edge sandwiching white band between a dark edge to the underwing-coverts. When soaring, pale band on underwing very noticeable. Underwing-coverts brown with white spots, and tail has black and white bands. At rest, dark coloration, spots on breast and to lesser extent wings, yellow cere and bare yellow legs distinguish it from similar-sized Changeable Hawk Eagle (*Spizaetus cirrhatus*). Immature has whitish underparts and dark upperparts with large pale spots. Sri Lankan race is endemic.

34

Shikra *Accipiter badius* 30–36 cm

Widely distributed and common. Occurs in heavily wooded and more open areas. Can be confused with scarce Besra (*Accipiter virgatus*) and Crested Goshawk (*Accipiter trivirgatus*). Male Shikra has grey upperparts, red eye and underparts finely barred rufous. Female similar but larger, with brownish-grey upperparts and orange eye. Immature has brown upperparts and dark spots on underparts; eye colour changes from grey to yellow. Shikra separated from Besra by grey face grading into white throat, narrower throat line, fine barring on underparts (broad and vertical on breast, and horizontal on belly in Besra). Crested Goshawk larger with streaks on breast, and fine black bars on tibia coverts. Juveniles of all three species have brown streaks on underparts formed by spots melding together. Gives screaming call *iheeya, iheeya*.

(Above right) *male;* (right) *sub adult*

Black Eagle *Ictinaetus malayensis* 69–81 cm

An unmistakable raptor. Whereas Crested Serpent Eagle (*Spilornis cheela*) soars, this species tends to follow contours of forested hills. Readily identified by overall black plumage except for yellow feet and cere. Indistinct barring on underwing and undertail only visible at close range. Has distinctive long-tailed and long-winged appearance in flight, with wings narrower at base and widening out to separated tips. Seen head on, the primaries can be seen curling upwards. Does occur locally in the lowlands where suitable hilly outcrops are found such as at Ritigala, but is commonest in the higher hills hunting over forest. In the breeding season it utters a moderately loud whistle *keeeu*.

35

Booted Eagle *Hieraaetus pennatus* 45–55 cm

Tim Loseby

A medium-large eagle with broad, longish and rather rounded wings, and square-ended tail in flight. Pale and dark colour morphs occur, but dark morph birds are rare. Both have brown upperparts with paler upperwing-coverts. Pale birds have underparts and underwing-coverts whitish, rest of underwing blackish with paler inner primaries and unmarked darker grey tail. Dark birds have brown underparts, dark underwing with paler inner primaries and browner tail. Regular but scarce winter migrant to the country.

Changeable Hawk Eagle (Crested Hawk-Eagle)
Spizaetus cirrhatus 60–75 cm

T.S.U. de Zylva

Common larger raptor of dry lowlands; less common in wet lowlands and up to higher hills. Recognized by its very upright crest and brown upperparts, and mostly whitish underparts. Much variation in plumage according to age. Adult shows dark streaking on underparts. Juvenile 'clean'-looking with pale face, brown and whitish upperparts, and unmarked whitish underparts. Plumage gradually darkens with age, and this results in distinct plumage variations in the species. Immatures often perch in trees and utter their call, a rising, ringing *ki, ki, ki, ki, ki, ki, ki, ki, keek*. Adults call *klee, klek*. Soars less frequently than Crested Serpent Eagle (*Spilornis cheela*), more often perching on bare trees in open plains.

Common Kestrel *Falco tinnunculus* 32–35 cm

Male Common Kestrel is an unmistakable small falcon. The majority of kestrels are winter migrants and they are sometimes seen in towns during migration. Birds of resident population are smaller than wintering race, and rare, restricted to higher hills. Male has grey head and tail, with a black sub-terminal band, chestnut upperparts with dark spots, and pale underparts with spots and broken streaks. Female has rufous-brown upperparts with dark streaks on head and pale underparts, and fine dark bars on rest of upperparts. Both sexes have thick dark streak below eye. Juvenile similar to female. It has a characteristic habit of hovering to hunt for prey.

Tim Loseby

Shaheen Falcon *Falco peregrinus peregrinator* 38–44 cm

Gehan De Silva Wijeyeratne

(Vulnerable). Shaheen Falcon is the local resident race of Peregrine Falcon (*F. peregrinus*). A rather small and a powerful-looking falcon which has blackish upperparts, rufous underparts with fine, dark streaks and white on throat. Complete black face mask is sharply demarcated from white throat. It has distinctive rufous underwing-coverts. Differs in all these features from paler Peregrine, which is a scarce winter migrant. The Shaheen is uncommon but found throughout the island, frequenting rock outcrops and rocky mountains. Sigiriya is a well-known site for it.

Jungle Bush Quail *Perdicula asiatica* 16–17 cm

Eric Lott

(Endangered). This quail is local, being restricted to the grasslands in the drier eastern slopes and foothills of the central mountain massif. The brick-red coloration and strongly contrasting facial pattern in both sexes enable easy identification. Male is strongly barred black and white unlike female. Like all quails this bird sticks to ground cover and is usually hard to see until flushed. The facial pattern distinguishes it from the more widespread Barred Button-quail. Lives in bevies outside the breeding season.

Grey Francolin (Indian Grey Partridge)
Francolinus pondicerianus 31–33 cm

Tim Loseby

Common ground bird of dry scrublands in the north-western coastal belt, found northwards from Chilaw. Rather shy, living in small groups or in pairs. Its far-carrying, rather sweet song, a continuous *ki-kee-kyek, ki-kee-kyek* is usually heard in the mornings and evenings, when it normally comes out into open areas for feeding. Another call is *kiko, kiko...* A large quail which has an attractive plumage pattern of brown blotches and fine barring on grey background. The black-edged brown throat contrasts with the greyer body.

Blue-breasted Quail *Coturnix chinensis* 13–15 cm

Eric Lott

Well-known small quail due its popularity as a cagebird. Male is brightly coloured, and flocks are captured and kept as pets. Shy and retiring in the wild, so seen infrequently. It lives in pairs or in small groups in paddy fields and damp grassy habitats, and is locally distributed throughout the island. Male attractively coloured with bluish-grey and maroon on body, a black throat and large white patch on ear-coverts giving a boldly patterned face. Female mainly pale yellowish-brown with dark markings. Told from female Rain Quail (*Coturnix coromandelica*) by barring not streaking on underparts, and a less clear, pale eye-brow.

* Sri Lanka Spurfowl *Galloperdix bicalcarata* 34 cm

T.S.U. de Zylva

(Vulnerable) Endemic. An extremely shy ground bird, inhabiting undergrowth of thick forests of lowlands and hills of wet zone, where it is fairly common. Found locally in some tall evergreen forests in dry zone. Male has red face and black and reddish-brown body with white spots. Female brown without distinct markings. Pairs often duet in the morning with a loud, ringing call, but are very elusive and difficult to see. The male's even *hu-hu-hu-hu* and female's rising *whi-whi-whi-whee* whistles are repeated many times. Occasionally may be seen feeding along or crossing trails. Kitulgala and Sinharaja are good places to look for this species where the undergrowth is more open, or at open areas at forest edge.

* Sri Lanka Junglefowl *Gallus lafayettii*
66–73 cm (male), 35–36 cm (female)

T.S.U. de Zylva

Endemic. Found throughout the island. A ground dweller, preferring forests and adjoining scrubs and plantations. Fairly common in suitable habitats and, although shy, frequently feeds in the open. Easiest to see in dry zone. The cock's loud *chok, chaw-choyik* is heard especially in the mornings. Often seen in family parties. A game drive in one of the southern national parks will usually locate this bird. Unlike glossy black and orange-yellow male, female is drab brown, and reminiscent of male Sri Lanka Spurfowl (*Galloperdix bicalcarata*) but has clear off-white bars on the wings, and yellowish legs and beak.

Indian Peafowl *Pavo cristatus*
180–230 cm (male), 90–100 cm (female)

T.S.U. de Zylva

The male with his long train of feathers is a spectacular sight in jungle areas of the low country dry zone. Female has green neck, brown upperparts and tail, without the train. Full-grown juvenile resembles female. Small flocks, often of females and immatures, sometimes accompanied by a male, are encountered in the national parks. Its far-carrying trumpet-like call *ka-aww* is a characteristic sound of the dry zone jungles. Courting males raise the 'tail' into a fan and dance around females with quivering wings.

Barred Buttonquail (Barred Bustard-Quail)
Turnix suscitator 13–15 cm

T.S.U. de Zylva

The 'quail' most likely to be seen, as it scurries across the road. Common in the grasslands of the low country dry zone, usually found in pairs. It is not rare in suitable habitats in the wet zone and the hills. Female larger and more brightly coloured, and has a black 'bib'. In this species, the normal role of the sexes is reversed. Female courts male; uttering a long purring call which sounds like a distant motorcycle. Male incubates the eggs.

Slaty-legged Crake (Banded Crake) *Rallina eurizonoides* 25 cm

T.S.U. de Zylva

A rather uncommon winter migrant found in forest habitats in hilly areas. Often seen in gardens near Colombo on its arrival on the island. Shy and solitary, keeping within cover in the forest. Becomes active towards dusk, when it sometimes utters a long-drawn, rattling *krrrrr...* and may be seen near water habitats in the forests. An unmistakable crake with its distinctive plumage and its preference for forest habitats. Male has chestnut head, neck and breast, olive-brown upperparts, underparts distinctly barred with black and white, and grey legs. Female resembles male but crown and hindneck are browner.

41

White-breasted Waterhen *Amaurornis phoenicurus* 32 cm

T.S.U. de Zylva

The commonest rail on the island, found in marshes, where its harsh *kwaar, kwaar... korowak korowak..* call is frequently heard. Overall blackish upperparts contrast sharply with white face, throat and breast, and chestnut belly and vent. Generally shy and usually in pairs. It occasionally erupts from tangled vegetation to fly short distances, before dropping into cover again. Can be seen in open areas, even in home gardens. Juvenile small and black; older immature nearly as large as adult and mostly blackish with some dusky white on breast.

Common Moorhen *Gallinula chloropus* 30–35 cm

T.S.U. de Zylva

A blackish waterbird usually found swimming among aquatic vegetation in lakes, tanks, marshes etc. Fairly common resident on water bodies in the lowlands. Blackish-grey overall with distinct white lines on flanks bordering the wings, white on undertail-coverts, and red on base of beak and frontal shield. May be confused with male Watercock (*Gallicrex cinerea*) in breeding plumage, which occurs in the same habitat but is usually a retiring bird. Watercock lacks Common Moorhen's white markings. Usually seen in pairs. Immature dull and brownish with pale markings rather than white in adult.

Purple Swamphen (Purple Coot) *Porphyrio porphyrio* 43 cm

T.S.U. de Zylva

A spectacular, brightly coloured bird. Blue overall with red beak and frontal shield and a striking white vent that is exposed by the regularly jerked tail. Common and readily seen in lowland marshes. Juvenile small and black; older immature larger and greyish. It utters a loud *kreek, krick, krick...* and a honking *aah, aah.*

Common Coot *Fulica atra* 36–40 cm

Gehan de Silva Wijeyeratne

An uncommon and unmistakable waterbird which mainly inhabits the tanks in the north of the island. Occasionally found on tanks elsewhere in the country. Plumage overall blackish; white beak and frontal shield makes this bird very distinctive. Often seen swimming in small groups. Until recently, Common Coot was a very rare bird in Sri Lanka, but it is now established in tanks in the Anuradhapura area. Strongly territorial, frequently engaging in disputes. Utters a metallic *chink*, often whilst swimming towards a rival.

43

Pheasant-tailed Jacana *Hydrophasianus chirurgus*
29–31 cm (plus 25 cm tail)

T.S.U. de Zylva

This distinctive, long-tailed waterbird is a familiar sight and sound of the marshes, and utters a range of calls: a loud *kawoorrk, kawoorrk...*; *krrrr, krrrr* and mewing sounds. After breeding, jacanas lose their attractive plumage and long tail, becoming drab with brownish upperparts and white underparts; a dark line runs from face down to breast band, along neck on either side, with some yellow retained on neck. Juvenile similar to non-breeding adult but has chestnut-brown on crown and lacks yellow on neck. In flight has a contrasting wing pattern with black-edged white wings. Fairly common resident in wetlands of the low country.

Greater Painted-snipe (Painted Snipe)
Rostratula benghalensis 23–28 cm

T.S.U. de Zylva

Largely nocturnal bird, but can be seen, often in flight, when flushed during the day. May be seen in pairs at the marshy edge of a lake or in low cover in a wetland. The conspicuous white eyebrow, white 'racing stripe' on the strongly patterned body and decurved beak makes confusion unlikely with any other wader. The appearance of the sexes is reversed in this bird, with male smaller and duller than female. Found throughout the lowlands to the lower hills.

44

Black-winged Stilt *Himantopus himantopus* 35–40 cm

T.S.U. de Zylva

An elegant wader with pink legs, black wings, white body and thin black beak. Common resident in wetland habitats throughout dry lowlands, and visits wet lowlands during the migratory season. Usually found in small flocks, birds keep in touch with a rather nasal call *gnaak, gnaak*. Female has brownish upperback and sometimes grey on head and hindneck. Immature similar to female but always has dark grey on head and grey on hindneck. Some melanistic birds show black on the hindneck or on both head and hindneck, and thus resemble races in Australia and America. In flight, pink legs trail behind unmarked black wings.

Pied Avocet *Recurvirostra avosetta* 42–45 cm

T.S.U. de Zylva

This delicate and graceful wader is a scarce winter visitor. The Avocet's upcurved bill and bluish legs (which usually look dark in the field) identify it. Feeds in shallow water, sweeping its bill actively from side to side, searching for invertebrates. Occurs in small flocks on breeding grounds; in Sri Lanka solitary individuals are likely.

45

Crab-plover *Dromas ardeola* 38–41 cm

Gehan de Silva Wijeyeratne

An unmistakable, large, black and white wader with heavy, short, black beak and long, bluish legs. Smaller than familiar Great Thick-knee (*Esacus recurvirostris*) which it somewhat resembles in general shape. A scarce resident, confined to the northern coasts and an occasional visitor to other coastal areas. Occurs solitarily, in pairs, or in small flocks. This bird has very unusual nesting habits for a shorebird in that it burrows into a sand bank, beside a beach.

Eurasian Thick-knee (Stone-Curlew)
Burhinus oedicnemus 40–44 cm

T.S.U. de Zylva

A large, brown bird found mainly in the lowlands in dry open scrubland habitats close to water. It lives in pairs and is a rather uncommon resident in the dry zone and even scarcer in the wet zone. It is largely nocturnal in habits, and rests under a bush during the day. Resting birds are easily overlooked due to their cryptic plumage. The heavily streaked body and small beak easily distinguish it from Great Thick-knee (*Esacus recurvirostris*). The call, usually uttered at night, is a series of *cur-lee, cur-lee* calls, loud at first but becoming gradually more soft.

46

Great Thick-knee (Great Stone-Plover)
Esacus recurvirostris 49–54 cm

T.S.U. de Zylva

A large sandy-brown bird with soft plumage. A rather uncommon resident which frequents wet habitats, mainly in coastal areas, but is less abundant at large inland tanks in the dry zone. It lives in pairs but small congregations are not unusual. The lack of streaking, larger beak and dark line on the face separate this species from Eurasian Thick-knee (*Burhinus oedicnemus*). It is active mainly at night, and its series of even, high-pitched, rather sweet whistles carry a great distance.

Small Pratincole (Little Pratincole) *Glareola lactea* 16–19 cm

T.S.U. de Zylva

A small, sandy-brown shorebird, tern-like in shape. Short, black beak is red at base. Often found resting on ground by water, in saltpans and lagoons and also by inland tanks in the dry zone. Smallest and palest of the pratincoles, being smaller than Little Tern (*Sterna albifrons*). Overall pale sandy in colour. However, black and white flight feathers give wing a distinctive pattern in flight. It hawks for insects in flight. Its short, cackling call is uttered mainly while flying. Usually found in flocks, but the birds may often be scattered over a large area. An uncommon resident preferring the dry zone, mostly in the coastal areas. Runs in short spurts, reminiscent of a plover.

Little Ringed Plover *Charadrius dubius* 14–17 cm

T.S.U. de Zylva

A small brown and white shorebird which frequents dry, muddy or grassy areas by water. Fairly common resident in dry lowlands, it also appears in the wet zone when residents are supplemented by winter visitors. In breeding plumage, black band appears on head, face and breast, yellow eye-ring becomes very prominent, and yellow legs become brighter. Non-breeding bird duller, without black head and face bands, and with brown breast band. Immature similar to non-breeding adult. Kentish Plover (*Charadrius alexandrinus*) similar, but has incomplete breast band, blackish legs and lacks yellow eye-ring. The lack of white wingbar, and presence of yellow eye-ring and legs are diagnostic for separating it from Ringed Plover (*Charadrius hiaticula*), a scarce migrant.

Ringed Plover *Charadrius hiaticula* 18–20 cm

T.S.U. de Zylva

A scarce migrant that is probably overlooked amongst large flocks of other waders. Recorded mainly from the south, but this is probably due to amount of observer coverage, as there is potentially suitable habitat throughout the lowlands, especially in the drier areas. Similar to Little Ringed Plover (*Charadrius dubius*) but is larger and dumpier with a white wingbar which Little Ringed Plover lacks. It does not have the prominent yellow eye-ring of Little Ringed. The beak has an orange-yellow base.

48

Kentish Plover *Charadrius alexandrinus* 15–17 cm

T.S.U. de Zylva

A rather uncommon resident found near the water in dry lowlands. The local population is strengthened by winter migrants, which are also found in wet lowlands. It has brownish-grey upperparts, white hind collar, and snowy white underparts with black marking on sides of breast. Male has black markings on head, and those of female are brown. Immatures are dull and resemble female. Differs from Little Ringed Plover (*Charadrius dubius*) by lack of yellow on the beak, eye ring or legs, a short, incomplete breast band and a faint wingbar in flight; from Lesser Sand Plover (*Charadrius mongolus*) by white hind collar and small breast patches.

Lesser Sand Plover *Charadrius mongolus* 19–21 cm

T.S.U. de Zylva

Common migrant that arrives in large numbers, mainly throughout dry coastal areas. Some immatures remain in the dry zone beyond the migratory season. Non-breeding bird dull brown and white. It has a broad, brown, usually incomplete breast band. This nondescript plumage is replaced by chestnut collar and black markings on face as it assumes breeding plumage. Unless seen together, this species may be hard to separate from Greater Sand Plover (*Charadrius leschenaultii*), a scarce winter migrant. The latter is larger, and has a heavy beak and pale legs usually with a greenish or yellowish tinge.

49

Greater Sand Plover (Large Sand Plover)
Charadrius leschenaultii 22–25 cm

Gehan de Silva Wijeyeratne

At first glance similar to Lesser Sand Plover (*Charadrius mongolus*); larger size not apparent unless the two species are seen together. Greater can be told apart by its longer and heavier beak, flattened crown, and 'longer' legs as it shows more of the tibia. The legs look dull yellow or greenish-grey. Both species are found in similar habitats, and often one or two Greaters are found alongside Lessers. Largely silent, but occasionally utters a *creek creek*. It is a scarce but regular winter migrant. Black on face and chestnut on breast in breeding plumage.

Caspian Plover *Charadrius asiaticus* 18–20 cm

Ismeth Raheem

A long-winged sand plover with pale legs. More elegant and longer-necked than Greater Sand Plover (*Charadrius leschenaultii*) which it resembles in non-breeding plumage, but Caspian has a broad, complete, greyish-brown breast band. It also has a pale face and a broad buffy supercilium, quite unlike those of Lesser (*Charadrius mongolus*) and Greater Sand Plovers. In breeding plumage, its face and supercilium are white with brownish eye-stripe, and the breast band is deep orange-chestnut with a black line at the lower border. Female, in all plumages, is more like non-breeding male. Leg colour varies from greenish-yellow to green-ish-grey. A rare but regular winter migrant to the coastal areas.

Pacific Golden Plover (Asiatic Golden Plover)
Pluvialis fulva 23–26 cm

Fairly common winter migrant. Winter plumage is buff and brown with yellow spangling on upperparts. Resembles winter-plumaged Grey Plover (*Pluvialis squatarola*), but has pale armpit in flight (black in Grey), a small beak and slimmer build. Prior to departure, birds assume breeding plumage with underparts from face down to vent turning deep black, and brighter yellow and black spangling on upperparts. Found mainly in dry zone lowlands; many suitable wet zone plains have been used for agriculture. Tends to gather in flocks, mainly on grassy habitats. Feeding birds often run a small distance, pause and peck. Flocks in flight utter a musical whistling *tu-wee, tu-wee*.

T.S.U. de Zylva

Grey Plover *Pluvialis squatarola* 27–30 cm

Eric Lott

Uncommon winter migrant, which spreads throughout coastal areas, but is found largely in dry zone. In winter plumage a greyish bird with spangled upperparts and whitish underparts. Wintering birds have a dark ear spot, and compared with Pacific Golden Plover (*Pluvialis fulva*) a thicker bill and chunkier build. In breeding plumage, assumed before departure, spangling on upperparts becomes more defined with dark grey and white, and underparts from face to vent turn deep black. The black armpit visible in flight is diagnostic in all plumages. It occurs singly or in small numbers but feeds alone.

51

Yellow-wattled Lapwing *Vanellus malabaricus* 26–28 cm

T.S.U. de Zylva

An attractive dry zone bird, found in driest plains, sometimes far from water, unlike Red-wattled Lapwing (*Vanellus indicus*) which favours damp areas. Black cap, brown breast and large yellow wattles at base of beak easily separate it from latter species. Often seen in pairs, standing motionless during the heat of the day. It mostly prefers the arid coastal areas but some birds are also found in dry inland areas. Visitors are most likely to see this bird in Ruhuna and Bundala National Parks. When disturbed, it utters a preliminary *kikiki* followed by a loud *keee-eeu*.

Red-wattled Lapwing *Vanellus indicus* 32–35 cm

T.S.U. de Zylva

A common bird throughout the lowlands, but less so in the hills. Found wherever the ground is damp, in marshes, wewas (tanks), paddy fields, grass flats or ditches. It has very small red wattles on its face unlike in Yellow-wattled Lapwing (*Vanellus malabaricus*). It lives in pairs, but sometimes a considerable number may congregate. It is sometimes known by the onomatopoeic name of *Did-he-do-it*, from its loud call. In flight shows a striking black and white wing pattern.

Sanderling *Calidris alba* 18–21 cm

Gehan de Silva Wijeyeratne

A small whitish wader often seen running along the edges of the waves on the sea shore. Usually found in flocks, feeding at the sea's edge or at a nearby lagoon. Mainly seen in winter plumage. Wintering birds have pure white underparts and greyer upperparts with fine dark streaks. In breeding plumage, upperparts are mottled rufous brown. Sanderling is an uncommon winter migrant to the island. In suitable habitats such as Chilaw Sand Spit, flocks of 40 birds or more may be seen mixing with other shore birds. It runs up and down, on its short black legs, following the ebb and flow of incoming waves.

Little Stint *Calidris minuta* 13–15 cm

T.S.U. de Zylva

The smallest common wader on mudflats and salt pans in the dry coastal areas. Flocks actively feed at the water's edge. In non-breeding plumage has brownish-grey feathers with dark centres on upperparts and whitish underparts. In breeding plumage neck, breast and upperparts rufous and feathers on upperparts have dark brown centres. Furthermore, a yellowish line on either side forms a large 'V' on upper back. Legs and beak are black in all seasons. A common winter migrant mainly to the dry coastal areas, and uncommon or rare elsewhere in the lowlands. Rather wary and easily put up on approach.

Temminck's Stint *Calidris temminckii* 13–15 cm

Gehan de Silva Wijeyeratne

Regular but scarce migrant. Often mixes with flocks of Little Stint (*Calidris minuta*) and other small waders. Spreads out around the coast, especially in the dry zone where it can find suitable muddy estuarine habitats. Easily distinguished from other stints by its yellowish legs. Its plumage pattern is often likened to that of a miniature Common Sandpiper (*Actitis hypoleucos*). It has a dark, diffuse patch enveloping the throat and breast. It shows much less mottling and streaking than other stints and has a 'cleaner cut' appearance. Occurs in the coastal strip along Chilaw and Puttlam, and in the arid strip around Hambantota.

Curlew Sandpiper *Calidris ferruginea* 18–23 cm

T.S.U. de Zylva

One of the most abundant winter visitors that spreads throughout the salt pans and estuarine areas in the low country, especially in the dry zone. Small flocks are often seen feeding on grassy plains in coastal areas some distance away from its favourite wet habitats. The slightly decurved tip to the bill and uniform brownish-grey colour distinguish it from all other similar-sized waders. Very similar to Dunlin (*Calidris alpina*), which is an occasional rare migrant. However, unlike Curlew Sandpiper, Dunlin has a dark line through the white rump, visible in flight.

Broad-billed Sandpiper *Limicola falcinellus* 16–18 cm

Tim Loseby

A small, active, stint-like wader with a broad, longish beak, slightly downcurved near tip. Slightly larger than Little Stint (*Calidris minuta*), with a whiter appearance in winter plumage. Curlew Sandpiper (*Calidris ferruginea*), which has a similar-shaped beak, is larger and has uniform upperparts and a slender beak. Broad-billed Sandpiper has a broader white supercilium split over the eye on the forehead, giving it a peculiar, double-supercilium appearance. This feature is very distinct in breeding plumage when upperparts turn darker. A rare winter migrant, generally found singly or with a few others in flocks of small common waders; however, occasionally occurs in large flocks.

Buff-breasted Sandpiper *Tryngites subruficollis* 18–20 cm

T.S.U. de Zylva

A very rare winter migrant from North America. This sandpiper prefers grass flats by water. It has a buff face, neck and breast, and buff fringes to dark feathers on upperparts imparting a strong scaly effect. White underwing-coverts are distinct in flight. Beak is black and legs are orangish-yellow. No plumage changes occur between the seasons. Ruff (*Philomachus pugnax*), a rather common migrant is similar in appearance to this sandpiper, but is larger and usually wades in water. In shape Buff-breasted Sandpiper is more reminiscent of a plover than a sandpiper.

55

Ruff *Philomachus pugnax* 26–32 cm (male), 20–25 cm (female)

A somewhat out-of-proportion, almost comical look characterises the Ruff. A slightly de-curved blunt-tipped beak, a heavy body with 'scaly' feathers and orange-yellow legs distinguish the bird. This species leaves Sri Lanka for its breeding grounds before developing the collar of feathers which gives it its name. Birds close to breeding plumage are richer brown and maintain 'scaling' on body feathers. A regular but not abundant visitor, mixing with other waders, typically in the dry lowlands. As a medium-sized wader, Ruffs stand out from the large mixed flocks of waders in which they occur.

Common Snipe *Gallinago gallinago* 25–27 cm

A scarce winter visitor. May be found anywhere in wet habitats, but is most likely to be encountered on weed-fringed lakes in the lowlands. Snipe are difficult to separate in the field. Common Snipe has dark brown wing-coverts which do not contrast with rest of wing and upperparts. In Common Snipe, the line through the eye is thicker than the supercilium at the point of convergence at the base of the bill. In flight, it shows a dark upperwing with distinct white trailing edge on secondaries, very faint in Pintail Snipe. The pale underwing has contrasting pale bars.

Pintail Snipe *Gallinago stenura* 25–27 cm

T.S.U. de Zylva

The commonest wintering snipe. Occurs in any wet habitat with short grass, including paddy fields. Snipe are easily overlooked as they remain motionless, blending in perfectly with the vegetation. In the field, snipe can be difficult to distinguish, with the exception of the small, rare Jack Snipe (*Lymnocryptes minimus*) which has a unique facial pattern. Pintail and scarce Common Snipe (*Gallinago gallinago*) share same habitats and are very similar. Pintail's dark eye stripe is narrower than buff supercilium at point of convergence at the bill. In flight differs from Common Snipe by uniform darker grey underwing and lack of distinct white trailing edge to wings.

Black-tailed Godwit *Limosa limosa* 36–44 cm

T.S.U. de Zylva

A large wader with a long beak, sometimes found in large numbers in coastal areas. Fairly common winter visitor. Usually present as scattered individuals in dry lowlands, although lately it is increasingly seen in small flocks. From scarcer Bar-tailed Godwit (*Limosa lapponica*), best distinguished by uniform brownish-grey upperparts, and in flight by the broad white wingbar and black band on the tail. It also has a slightly upturned beak. In breeding plumage, head neck and breast become rufous with dark bars on belly, and grey upperparts have some rufous spotting.

Bar-tailed Godwit *Limosa lapponica* 36–41 cm

Tim Loseby

Scarce winter migrant to coastal areas, that can be mistaken for Black-tailed Godwit (*Limosa limosa*) which arrives in greater numbers. The absence of a white wingbar, and the tail being black and white barred instead of completely black, are diagnostic but only obvious in flight. On the ground, Bar-tailed has a more upturned beak and has distinctly dark streaked grey upperparts in winter plumage. In breeding plumage, head, neck and all underparts become rufous, and the dark upperparts are spotted rufous.

Eurasian Curlew *Numenius arquata* 50–60 cm

T.S.U. de Zylva

An uncommon winter visitor that occurs throughout the lowlands. Most likely to be seen in the dry lowlands where relatively large open grasslands and meadows are found in protected areas. Occasionally it is seen on the shoreline. The long, downcurved beak and large size make confusion only possible with Whimbrel (*Numenius phaeopus*). The lack of crown stripes and longer beak identify Curlew.

Common Redshank *Tringa totanus* 27–29 cm

T.S.U. de Zylva

Common migrant arriving in good numbers. The red legs and red base of beak together with a strong white wingbar makes identification easy. In flight, white on back and rump contrasts with darker fore-wings. Immature has yellowish legs. It is quite a vocal wader and its fluting call is often heard in the salt pans (lewayas) in the south. The call is a flute-like *tew-wew-wit*; sometimes only the first one or two syllables are uttered.

Marsh Sandpiper *Tringa stagnatilis* 22–25 cm

T.S.U. de Zylva

A common wader that takes up winter residence throughout the lowlands. It can be seen from estuarine mangrove habitats to man-made artificial lakes fringed with wet meadows. The pale body and dark pencil-thin beak identify it from other waders. Although it shares similar plumage to Greenshank, the latter has a heavier, upturned beak. Often seen wading in water up to its belly; it also swims. The call is a sharp whistle *tiu*, sometimes repeated in rapid succession.

59

Common Greenshank *Tringa nebularia* 30–34 cm

A regular migrant that disperses throughout the lowlands, mainly in the dry zone where suitable estuarine habitats are found. Pale overall and may be confused with Marsh Sandpiper (*Tringa stagnatilis*), but easily distinguished by relatively chunky upturned beak and stouter build. Usually seen at the water's edge or wading in shallow water probing the mud. The flight-call is a flute-like *twee-twee-twee, wee-tu, wee-tu-tu*.

Green Sandpiper *Tringa ochropus* 21–24 cm

A migrant that disperses throughout the island. It may even turn up in public parks in Nuwara Eliya away from typical wader habitats in the lowlands. In flight, it looks almost black and white as the dark, plain wings contrast with white tail and rump. The tail tip is faintly barred but this is not always obvious. Confusion is possible with Wood Sandpiper (*Tringa glareola*), but is has much darker upperparts with smaller pale spots and is shorter in the legs. Also, pale eye-brow does not extend behind the eye.

Wood Sandpiper *Tringa glareola* 19–21 cm

T.S.U. de Zylva

A common migrant that occurs in wet places throughout the low-lands. Shows heavily flecked upperparts and a clear supercilium. Often seen as solitary birds, occasionally in small flocks. In flight upperwings are fairly uniform and contrast with white rump and weakly barred tail. Upperwing pattern is reminiscent of Green Sandpiper (*Tringa ochropus*) but lacks the strong contrast of the latter, and supercilium extends behind eye.

Common Sandpiper *Actitis hypoleucos* 19–21 cm

T.S.U. de Zylva

A common migrant that spreads throughout the country from the lowlands to the highlands. Most likely to be seen on the edges of tanks in the dry zone but also found in water bodies, canals, etc. in the wet zone. It has a distinctive stiff-winged flight and shows a white wingbar. It bobs up and down constantly. The white of the underparts curves around the shoulder of the wing. Green Sandpiper (*Tringa ochropus*) lacks this feature, and has fine pale spots on darker upperparts; and in flight it lacks the white wingbar. The call, uttered in flight, is a high-pitched, *twee, wee, wee*.

61

Ruddy Turnstone (Turnstone) *Arenaria interpres* 21–24 cm

T.S.U. de Zylva

A common, but not abundant, winter visitor that disperses throughout coastal areas. Its preferred habitat is rocky shore where it turns over seaweed, pebbles and debris in search of its invertebrate prey. In winter plumage is heavily mottled in browns which change to black and bright chestnut in breeding plumage. The birds are easily identified with their short beak and low body profile. In flight has a distinctive appearance with a white wingbar that curves around to run parallel to the body.

Red-necked Phalarope *Phalaropus lobatus* 17–19 cm

Eric Lott

A small whitish wader often found swimming with other waders in salt pans and lagoons near the sea. It feeds whilst swimming, often twisting sideways. This species also feeds in the open sea. In winter plumage its upperparts are grey and its face, neck and underparts are pure white. It has a very finely pointed black beak, and a black mark across the eye. In breeding plumage female brighter than male. Female shows dark grey upperparts with chestnut on sides of neck, buff stripes on back, and white underparts. Rare but regular winter migrant, in small numbers, to the south-eastern coastal areas.

(Common) Black-headed Gull *Larus ridibundus* 36–40 cm

Gehan de Silva Wijeyeratne

A scarce winter visitor that may be overlooked due to similarity with Brown-headed Gull (*Larus brunnicephalus*) which is a regular migrant. Adults of both species have red bills and legs, with black marks on face in winter plumage. The wing pattern differs. Black-headed has black border to whiter upperwing tip, smoky black primaries in underwing, and is a slimmer bird; Brown-headed has a black triangle with two small white circles on each wing tip. Immature has black tip to tail and variable amounts of brown on grey mantle.

Brown-headed Gull *Larus brunnicephalus* 42–46 cm

A common migrant that spreads throughout coastal areas. In some years may occur in good numbers, even on Beira Lake in Colombo. The chocolate brown head, distinct black triangle at wing tip with white 'mirror' and size distinguish this from all other migrant gulls. Care must be taken to distinguish it from the scarcer and smaller Black-headed Gull (*Larus ridibundus*) which can also have a chocolate brown head. The latter has a white leading edge to its narrower and more pointed wings. The call is a cawing *khaa*.

T.S.U. de Zylva

T.S.U. de Zylva

(Top) *summer;* (bottom) *winter plumage*

Gull-billed Tern *Gelochelidon nilotica* 35–38 cm

T.S.U. de Zylva

A common migrant that spreads thoughout the lowlands but is more likely to be encountered in the dry wetlands, especially close to coast. It is not as abundant as Whiskered Tern (*Chlidonias hybridus*). In winter plumage it can be separated from Whiskered Tern by its heavier build, thicker black bill and black ear spot. The primaries have a dark trailing edge, noticeable in flight. In breeding plumage a well-defined black cap replaces the dark ear spot. Occasionally utters *wik, kuwikkeewik* call.

Caspian Tern *Sterna caspia* 47–55 cm

T.S.U. de Zylva

The largest of the terns, and unmistakable due to its size and large red beak. In non-breeding plumage shows short black crest, black across eye and fine black streaks on head; shows complete black cap in breeding plumage. Legs black. Black on outer primaries of underwing is distinct in flight. It is a coastal bird preferring the dry zone. Often small flocks can be seen resting on the ground together with other terns. Regularly pairs visit tanks near the coast. A small population is resident and the majority are winter migrants. Its harsh cry *krwekiar* is repeated several times in flight.

64

Great Crested Tern (Large Crested Tern)
Sterna bergii 45–49 cm

The second largest tern in the island, with distinct crest on nape. It has a heavy yellow beak, deeply forked tail, dark grey upperparts, white underparts and black legs. Breeding birds have crown and crest uniform black, and forehead white. During winter, non-breeding birds have white crown with fine black streaks. The head pattern of immature is similar to that of non-breeding adults, and they have dull yellow beaks and browner upperparts. One of the few resident terns, confined to the coast, breeding on offshore islands and sometimes in remote coastal areas. Birds in display flight utter a harsh *kraak* repeatedly. Also known as Swift Tern.

Little Tern *Sterna albifrons* 22–24 cm

The smallest of the island's terns, it is resident in considerable numbers, mainly in the dry zone. Small size, yellow beak and black line on face distinguish it from all except Saunders's Tern (*Sterna saundersi*), which was formerly considered a subspecies of Little Tern. In breeding plumage, Saunders's Tern has white only on forehead without extending over eye, brownish-yellow legs and has a broad black leading edge on primaries. Little Tern is found in coastal habitats and occasionally on inland water bodies. Displaying birds constantly utter soft, chattering calls.

T.S.U. de Zylva

65

Roseate Tern *Sterna dougallii* 33–38 cm

A beautiful tern in breeding plumage: black cap, pale grey upperparts, rosy tinge on underparts and long white tail. The beak is black with some red at base; legs red. In non-breeding plumage, black on head reduces to white forehead and streaky fore crown, but usually remains on hind crown and nape; beak is black and legs dark red. A length of tail usually remains protruding beyond closed wing tips. A dark carpal bar on wings is less distinct than in non-breeding Common Tern (*Sterna hirundo*). Underparts generally whitish with variable rosy tinge. Breeding visitor to rocky islets off coast, only occasionally coming to shore. Rare during migration season.

T.S.U. de Zylva

Common Tern *Sterna hirundo* 31–35 cm

T.S.U. de Zylva

In winter plumage Common Tern resembles Whiskered Tern (*Chlidonias hybridus*), but is larger, has longer beak and longer, more deeply-forked tail. In winter both species occur together, sometimes in large numbers, in coastal areas. Size, head pattern and wing markings are useful to identify Common Terns in these flocks. In winter Common Tern has uniform black rear half of crown and nape, forming a black half-cap, which contrasts with rest of white head. Folded wings show distinct blackish bar at carpal joint. Upperparts greyer than Whiskered Tern, and underparts white. Breeding birds show full black cap, grey upperparts, red legs and red beak with blackish tip. Common Terns migrate in large numbers every year. Several pairs bred off east coast during 1980s.

66

Whiskered Tern *Chlidonias hybridus* 23–26 cm

Common migrant which disperses throughout the lowlands. Numbering in the thousands, there does not appear to be a body of water in the lowlands where this species is absent. Calls frequently as it tirelessly circles over a body of water plunging in occasionally to take a fish. On arrival, these terns are mainly white with black streaking on the crown. By departure, they have acquired a black cap and very dark underparts with a white stripe ('the whiskers') in between, and a red bill and legs. Soft, creaking call may be repeatedly uttered in flight.

Rock Pigeon (Rock Dove) *Columba livia* 33 cm

(Vulnerable). True wild Rock Pigeons are identical to feral grey pigeons with two dark bands on the wings. They are frequent in towns, villages and in domestic collections. Wild Rock Pigeons have a darker grey rump than feral pigeons but are otherwise similar. Rock Pigeons are rare and found on offshore rocky islets and sometime nesting in holes of dead trees in national parks, on eastern and south-eastern coasts. Also occurs at inland dams. Call is deep *coo, coo* of the domestic pigeon, and the courting male utters a low *wop, wop, woppera-woo-oo*.

* Sri Lanka Wood Pigeon *Columba torringtoni* 36 cm

T.S.U. de Zylva

(Endangered). Endemic. A scarce forest bird, sometimes found in well-wooded home gardens in the higher hills. Generally found singly or in pairs, but small flocks are not exceptional. Best observed in morning and evening when most active. May be seen roosting in shady trees in suitable habitats during the middle of the day. The deep, pigeon-type call *woo, woo* in the higher hills indicates this species, but Green Imperial Pigeon (*Ducula aenea*) occurs at lower elevations, and utters a similar call. Horton Plains National Park, Hakgala Botanic Gardens and Surrey Estate are good places to find this species. Makes seasonal movements to lower elevations and may be seen at Sinharaja and in the forest in Kandy area (Rosenheath, Hantana), in the lower hills.

Spotted Dove *Streptopelia chinensis ceylonensis* 30 cm

T.S.U. de Zylva

A common bird throughout the country, although more abundant in the dry lowlands. Utters a far-carrying, cooing call *kukroo, kukoor, koo, koo, koo*, a very familiar sound in most rural or uninhabited areas, heard also in some towns. It has a 'chess board' pattern on the hind neck. Often encountered sitting on roads in national parks. The Sri Lankan race is endemic.

68

Emerald Dove *Chalcophaps indica* 27 cm

A widespread, dainty pigeon preferring well-forested areas although it may be encountered feeding along roads in both wet and dry lowlands. A small green pigeon with black and white barring on the back, often seen flying swiftly between cover. Occasionally can be seen feeding on open trails. Call is a deep *hoo, hoo...*, each *hoo* preceded by a soft *tk* audible only at close range.

Orange-breasted Green Pigeon *Treron bicincta* 29 cm

(Left) *male;* (above) *female*

Common in the dry lowlands, sometimes mixing with the more common Pompadour Green Pigeon (*Treron pompadora*). The male is unmistakable with his beautiful purple and orange breast band. Female closely resembles female Pompadour, but has chestnut undertail-coverts compared with light yellow in female Pompadour. Both sexes also have grey hind neck, absent in Pompadour. The rather soft song of the male consists of a short, siren-like wail followed by *uh-uh, eh-eh-ehwoo, eh-eh-ehwoo, eh-eh-eh*.

★ Ceylon Green-pigeon *Treron pompadora* 27 cm

Gehan de Silva Wijeyeratne

Endemic. The commonest of the Green Pigeons, occurring in small flocks throughout the island up to the mid hills. In the dry lowlands large flocks may be seen more easily. Male has unmistakable maroon back. See Orange-breasted Green-pigeon (*Treron bicincta*) for details on separating females of the two species. Often seen in national parks. At times may occur in good numbers, and at other times may be virtually absent due to local migrations. Song is a beautiful, soft, modulated human-like whistle.

Green Imperial-pigeon *Ducula aenea* 42–47 cm

T.S.U. de Zylva

A common bird throughout the island wherever there are sizeable patches of forest and recently spreading into wooded town areas. Found both in the dry zone and the wet zone ascending up to the lower hills. In the hills, the call may be confused with that of endemic Ceylon Wood-pigeon (*Columba torringtonii*). Cannot be mistaken for any other pigeon on plumage with its green wings and back, and grey body and head. The undertail-coverts are chestnut. At a distance it shows little contrast. It has three very deep-toned songs, all frequently heard: *wok-wooor*, *wrooo* and *hmm, hmm, hm-hm-hm-hm*.

* Sri Lanka Hanging Parrot (Ceylon Lorikeet)
Loriculus beryllinus 14 cm

(Vulnerable). Endemic. The smallest member of the parrot family in Sri Lanka. Solitary birds often hurtle overhead uttering a loud, unmistakable high-pitched three-note call: *tchee-tchee-tchik*. Small size and green coloration makes them difficult to see when perched in tree tops. Occasionally feeds on low trees. Sexes similar with green body and red on crown and uppertail-coverts. Found in forests and adjoining well-wooded home gardens and plantations, from lowlands to hills at about 1200m. Also in pockets of wetter forest in the dry zone. Often seen in the Kitulgala Rest House garden and surrounding area. The garden of the Ratnaloka Tour Inn, Pompekele Forest in Ratnapura, Gilimale Forest and Sinharaja are also good sites. Found locally in intermediate forest around the Kandalama Wewa.

T.S.U. de Zylva

Alexandrine Parakeet *Psittacula eupatria* 48–58 cm

This species is found throughout the lowlands in small flocks, but is not as abundant as the somewhat smaller Rose-ringed Parakeet (*Psittacula krameri*). Easily overlooked, but the larger size, heavy-set red bill and red shoulder patch should distinguish it from Rose-ringed Parakeet. In flight, the different call and the long tail aids separation. Its call is somewhat similar to that of Rose-ringed, but is harsher and louder: a repeated, three-phrased, *kreeak, kreeyak, kreeyak*. It also utters a harsh *kreah* in flight.

T.S.U. de Zylva

Rose-ringed Parakeet (Ring-necked Parakeet)
Psittacula krameri 38–42 cm

By far the commonest parakeet in the lowlands. It is one of the few birds which is not protected as it is considered an agricultural pest. The birds often alight atop tall trees before vanishing, betrayed only by their shrill screaming *kyeeuk, kyeeuk* contact call. It has a similar-toned chattering call uttered at length. Small flocks can often be heard screeching overhead. It nests in tree burrows and competes for nest sites with barbets. Only the male has the rose collar. His face has a powder blue tinge.

T.S.U. de Zylva

Plum-headed Parakeet (Blossom-headed Parakeet)
Psittacula cyanocephala 34–36 cm

The smallest and most colourful of the parakeets, it is more likely to be encountered in the wet zone than the dry zone, where it occurs in small local populations. It is commonest in the hills and generally favours forest patches although flocks may be seen feeding in paddy fields. The call is an unmistakable, pretty *tuai* with 'i' higher in pitch, mostly uttered in flight. The female has a bluish-grey head and yellow collar. The yellow beak, yellow collar and white-tipped tail separate the female from other parakeets.

T.S.U. de Zylva

* Layard's Parakeet *Psittacula calthropae* 31 cm

(Vulnerable). Endemic. Uncommon species in forests and adjoining habitats in wet zone, from lowlands to about 1200m. Rather scarce and locally distributed in the forests of the drier foothills and adjoining areas. In the hills, flocks can be encountered in gardens and parks. Often seen in pairs or in small flocks flying high above the canopy. Their loud, harsh call *eek-ehk, ak* is uttered repeatedly. In flight this call, together with rather short tail, are diagnostic. Sometimes seen in bird waves, especially in Sinharaja. Edge habitats in Kitulgala and Sinharaja are good places to see this species, as is approach road from Veddagala to Sinharaja, Bodhinagala, Gilimale, and the Peradeniya Botanical Gardens. Can be observed within 40 km of Colombo (at Homagama), and within Peak Wilderness Sanctuary.

T.S.U. de Zylva

Pied Cuckoo (Pied Crested Cuckoo)
Clamator jacobinus 33 cm

T.S.U. de Zylva

This attractive, energetic bird is most likely to be seen in the scrub forest of the dry zone. However, it has a wide distribution and may even be found in the woods adjoining wetlands in the wet zone. Distinctive in its smart black and white plumage. It is seen singly or in pairs. Immatures have a buff tinge on the white areas. The song is a loud whistle *pee-u-pippew* repeated a few times.

Asian Koel (Indian Koel) *Eudynamys scolopacea* 40–44 cm

(Above) *male;* (right) *female*

A common garden bird found throughout the country. Both sexes have a striking red eye. Male all-black with pale beak, long tail and slimmer build that distinguishes it from both crows. Female heavily barred and spotted in brown and white. It is not uncommon to see this bird being pursued by crows. Local tradition has it that the koel's incessant calling heralds the Sinhala and Tamil New Year in April and it is known as 'New Year Cuckoo'. The male has two loud songs: a rapidly-repeated, rising *hweeyu-hweeyu-hweeyu...* and a pleasant, slow, rising *ku-oo-u, ku-oo-u...* with the middle syllable higher. Female's call is a quick, rising yelp *kik-kik-kik*.

Blue-faced Malkoha *Phaenicophaeus viridirostris* 39 cm

A bird of the dry zone scrub forests. An uncommon resident. It can be seen at the forest edges bordering villages and also visits village gardens. The pale bill, dark upper body and the white-tipped tail feathers are reminiscent of the Red-faced Malkoha (*Phaenicophaeus pyrrhocephalus*) which also occurs locally in the dry zone. However, the blue ring around the eye will identify this species. It is not as arboreal as is Red-faced Malkoha, and can be found threading its way through low bushes and trees.

74

Sirkeer Malkoha (Southern Sirkeer)
Phaenicophaeus leschenaultii 42 cm

T.S.U. de Zylva

(Vulnerable). A scarce resident of the dry zone scrub jungles. The best places to see it are the national parks like Ruhuna. A nondescript brown bird with a bright red beak, and a black line through the eye. Prefers to forage on the ground in similar fashion to Greater Coucal (*Centropus sinensis*). Like Blue-faced Malkoha (*Phaenicophaeus viridirostris*), may be seen foraging in low cover. It sometimes utters a repeated *kik, kik*.

* Green-billed Coucal *Centropus chlororhynchus* 43 cm

T.S.U. de Zylva

(Endangered). Endemic. A rare and elusive bird, confined to thick evergreen forests with dense undergrowth mainly of bamboo, or mixed with ferns and rattan, in the wet lowlands and mid hills up to 1,100m. Pairs maintain a territory throughout the year. They utter a deep, two syllable call, *hoop-oop*, the first syllable higher, also other deep calls and coughing sounds, and a somnolent *hmmm hmmm*. An undergrowth species, it often ascends to trees or flies into the open whilst calling to challenge rivals. Sometimes found in bird waves. Similar to Greater Coucal (*Centropus sinensis*) but distinguished by its beak which is ivory or pale green. The best place for seeing this species is Bodhinagala forest where its density is high (difficult recently). It occurs at Sinharaja in lower densities.

75

Greater Coucal (Common Coucal) *Centropus sinensis* 48 cm

T.S.U. de Zylva

Common and widely distributed in gardens and degraded forest. Not shy and often seen in gardens foraging for snails, lizards and other small animals. Sexes similar with glossy black body, chestnut wings and a striking red eye. Pairs keep in regular contact with whooping calls. The dark bill readily separates it from Green-billed Coucal (*Centropus chlororhynchus*). Also has brighter chestnut wings, and different sheen on head and neck. Can occur in similar habitats and care needs to be taken in distinguishing these species by call. Call is a familiar deep *hoop-oop-oop-oop-oop-oop*, sometimes in a duet of two different pitches. It also makes hissing and *chock* sounds.

Barn Owl *Tyto alba* 36 cm

Bandula Gunawardana

(Endangered). An unmistakable large owl with its heart-shaped white face and sparsely marked white underparts. Widespread but rare in the lowlands. Its presence is easily overlooked mainly due to lack of any loud and distinct calls like those of other owls. Utters high-pitched screech during breeding season. In Colombo and its suburbs it is found where suitable large, old buildings exist for roosting. Uses adjacent open areas to hunt for prey. Recent records indicate it may not be as rare as it was previously thought to be.

Oriental Bay Owl (Bay Owl) *Phodilus badius assimilis* 28 cm

(Critically Endangered). A very rare, medium-sized forest owl. Distributed in the lowlands up to the lower hills. Only a little more than a dozen sightings of this owl have been made to date. Rather similar in appearance to Barn Owl (*Tyto alba*), but has rich chestnut and buff upperparts and black, heart-shaped spots on pinkish-buff underparts. Strictly nocturnal and very shy. The voice of the local race of this owl is still not known, which may be one factor for the paucity of records. Nests in hollow trees.

T.S.U. de Zylva

Collared Scops Owl (Indian Scops Owl)
Otus bakkamoena 23 cm

A common and widespread owl up to 1,200 m, that can only be confused with scarcer and distinctly smaller Oriental Scops Owl (*Otus sunia*) which has yellow irides rather than brown. Its rather loud *wock ?* call with a 'questioning' tone is common even in urban areas where it is treated as the harbinger of bad luck. Often found in pairs. In daylight the lightly marked underparts can be seen as opposed to heavier markings on Oriental Scops Owl. Not shy, often allowing a close approach.

T.S.U. de Zylva

77

Oriental Scops Owl (Little Scops Owl) *Otus sunia* 17–19 cm

Lester Perera

(Vulnerable). A small forest owl with distinct ear tufts and yellow irides. It is the smallest owl in Sri Lanka. Occurs in two colour-forms: one is bright chestnut and the other is greyish-brown. Lives in pairs, each pair maintaining a fairly large territory. Territorial song is a loud repeated *tuk, tok-torok*, of which the first syllable is quieter than the last two. An uncommon resident distributed in forests almost throughout the island, but commoner in the dry zone.

Spot-bellied Eagle Owl (Forest Eagle Owl)
Bubo nipalensis 61 cm

Uditha Hettige

(Vulnerable). A favourite with visiting birders who make a special effort to see it. May be seen in wooded stands in dry zone national parks. It has a loud, long-drawn, sinister-sounding song *oooo-oh* with a nasal quality, usually repeated a few times, sometimes ending with loud gurgling sounds. Also utters short human-sounding hoot. Known as the Devil Bird on account of these calls. An uncommon forest resident throughout island. Brown eyes, black and white barred ear tufts, and blackish spots on white belly identify it. Brown Wood Owl (*Strix leptogrammica*) is nearly as large but shows barring and warm brown facial disk. Brown Fish Owl (*Ketupa zeylonensis*) is buff below with streaking, and has yellow eyes.

78

Brown Fish Owl *Ketupa zeylonensis* 54 cm

T.S.U. de Zylva

A common large owl of dry lowlands. The most likely of the large owls to be caught in the glare of the headlights at night, along a remote road. The yellow eyes and streaked buff underparts separate it from the other large owls. Roosts in large trees beside water. Deep, sad-sounding duet *oomp-ooomp-oomp* with one bird uttering the first and third syllables and its mate the higher-pitched second syllable.

* Chestnut-backed Owlet *Glaucidium castanonotum* 19–20 cm

T.S.U. de Zylva

(Vulnerable). Endemic. Fairly common small owl in forest and sometimes in adjoining well-wooded gardens, from lowlands to higher hills in the wet zone. Often heard calling from roost or seen hunting diurnally. Gives two far-carrying, prolonged sounds: a loud *kaow kaow*, and a soft *krook krook*... The threatening song is *krook krook* accelerating into *kaow kaow* and ending *kao-whap kao-whap*. Calling birds can be difficult to locate due to small size and cryptic coloration. Mornings and evenings best times to find it, when it is quite vocal. A pair maintains a territory throughout year, but may have several day roosts and may not occupy same roost on consecutive days. Seen regularly at Kitulgala and Sinharaja, but possible in almost any wet zone forest. Recorded in Bodhinagala, as well as Udawattakele and Rosenheath Hill forests in Kandy.

79

Brown Hawk Owl *Ninox scutulata* 30–32 cm

Chandima Kahandawala

One of the commonest owls, nearly the size of a crow. Its call is a familiar sound in the urban nightscape, wherever large old trees providing good cover have been spared the developer's axe. TV antennas and lamp posts are used as convenient watch points and territorial markers. It is active at dusk but can be overlooked when sitting on an antenna as it does not call until darkness has fallen. It has a long profile, unlike the typical dumpy owl profile. Its call is a distinctive loud *koo-ook, koo-ook* with the *ook* higher in pitch.

Brown Wood Owl *Strix leptogrammica* 46 cm

T.S.U. de Zylva

An uncommon but widespread owl found in wooded regions at all altitudes. Although a forest bird, it has adapted to well-wooded areas with human habitation. The distinct buff facial disks, lack of ear tufts and chestnut barring enable separation from the two other large owls, Forest Eagle Owl (*Bubo nipalensis*) and Brown Fish Owl (*Ketupa zeylonensis*). The call is a repeated, rather deep *hu-hu, hoo* with a sinister quality. This owl too is sometimes identified by villagers as the Devil Bird. Surrey Estate is a noted site.

Sri Lanka Frogmouth *Batrachostomus moniliger* 23 cm

T.S.U. de Zylva

This species is endemic to the Indian subcontinent and is sought after by birders. It frequents wet zone forests and is distributed to all but the higher hills. It not common anywhere, appearing to occur in low densities. Kitulgala, Bodhinagala and Sinharaja are the favoured locations for seeing these birds. They are not easy to locate as they look like the stub of a broken branch. The calls are a harsh *chaaak*, a liquid *klok-klok-klok...* and a simple descending whistle.

Crested Treeswift *Hemiprocne coronata* 21–24 cm

The long slender wings and long, pointed, deeply forked tail distinguish this species from swallows, the only likely confusion species. Also, the grey coloration can be seen when near. It is most likely to be seen in the dry lowlands where a small number of birds may be seen perched on an exposed branch of a tall tree. Female lacks chestnut cheek patch. The call is a nasal *gnew-gneek* often repeated in flight. In flight the crest is not seen; usually only erect when perched.

(Top) *male;*
(bottom) *female*

T.S.U. de Zylva

T.S.U. de Zylva

Indian Swiftlet (Indian Edible-nest Swift)
Collocalia unicolor 12cm

T.S.U. de Zylva

The second-smallest Sri Lankan swift, it is widely distributed throughout the island. Common in higher hills, and flocks often nest in railway tunnels and caves. The bird is at risk from nest collectors who destroy eggs and young. Despite its island-wide distribution, its nest colonies seem to be confined to wet zone especially in the hills. Its dumpy appearance with a notched tail distinguishes it from the more slender Asian Palm Swift (*Cypsiurus balasiensis*). House Swift (*Apus affinis*) is larger and has a white rump. Unlike other swifts, it is quiet in flight.

Malabar Trogon (Ceylon Trogon)
Harpactes fasciatus fasciatus 28 cm

T.S.U. de Zylva

Although found throughout forested areas in the lowlands and hills it is more likely to be seen in the lowland wet zone forests. The only trogon in Sri Lanka. Usually found in pairs; if one is seen the other is not likely to be far away. Male has striking red underparts, white breast-band and black head. Female orangish-brown with darker brown head. Usually joins bird waves. Often remains perched motionless, except for tail being flicked, before darting out to catch an insect. Calls: a pleasant *kyock, kyock* mostly by male and a soft, descending *trrr, trrr* mostly by female.

82

Stork-billed Kingfisher *Halcyon capensis* 38–41 cm

T.S.U. de Zylva

The largest of the Sri Lankan kingfishers, it is a distinctive bird with a heavy beak. Its loud, wailing *kyeeu-kiu, kyeeu-kiu*, with the first syllable higher, often betrays its presence beside rivers and streams before the bird is seen. It has also a loud laughing cry *khak-khak-khak-khak*. It is not shy and will visit well-wooded gardens but is commonest in good riverside habitat.

White-throated Kingfisher (White-breasted Kingfisher) *Halcyon smyrnensis* 28–30 cm

Probably the most familiar kingfisher on account of habit of perching on roadside telegraph wires. Regular visitor to home gardens where it catches grasshoppers and other invertebrates. It is rarely seen catching fish, tending to feed more on terrestrial invertebrates. It has a white throat and breast, chocolate on head and underparts, and a striking blue on upperparts. In flight, white panel at base of primaries contrasts with dark-tipped flight feathers and chestnut-shouldered blue upperwing. The upperwing

T.S.U. de Zylva

pattern in flight is similar to that of rare Black-capped Kingfisher (*Halcyon pileata*). It frequently draws attention to itself by a song uttered at rest, a whinnying *wi-hi-hi-hi-hi*. It also has a short *chik* call uttered while perched.

83

Black-capped Kingfisher *Halcyon pileata* 29–31 cm

T.S.U. de Zylva

A striking bird with black cap contrasting sharply with white collar, orangish underparts and purple-blue upperparts. In flight similar to common White-throated Kingfisher (*Halcyon smyrnensis*) as it shares large white upperwing patches against bluish upperparts. The black cap and white collar distinguish it. This is a rare migrant with at most only a few birds recorded each year. A bird may return to the same site in Sri Lanka year after year. It can turn up anywhere from mangroves, to rivers and lakes in the dry zone, but is never far from water.

Common Kingfisher *Alcedo atthis* 16 cm

T.S.U. de Zylva

A common and widespread bird though scarce at the highest elevations. Seemingly present at every village tank. The overall blue plumage and small size make confusion difficult except with rare Blue-eared Kingfisher (*Alcedo meninting*) that has blue rather than chestnut ear coverts. Common Kingfisher can conceal its chestnut ear coverts when it adopts a hunched posture, so care needs to be taken in separating the two. In Blue-eared, both sexes have orange in the black bill, and the orange is more extensive in the female. In Common, only female has orange, with male having an all-black bill. It utters a high-pitched *peek, peek* usually in flight.

Oriental Dwarf Kingfisher (Indian Three-toed Kingfisher) *Ceyx erithacus* 13–14 cm

T.S.U. de Zylva

The smallest and most beautifully coloured kingfisher in the island. A forest species which rarely spends time in the open except when flying from one forest patch to the other. Also occurs in well-wooded home gardens close to forest patches which it frequents. In the forest, in correct light conditions, its colours glisten like a small jewel against the green background. Its call is a high-pitched, and often repeated *kee, kee* usually uttered in flight. An uncommon resident distributed in the lowlands and up to about the mid hills.

Pied Kingfisher *Ceryle rudis* 29–31 cm

T.S.U. de Zylva

Boldly patterned black and white kingfisher with a distinctive habit of hovering before plunging in to catch a fish. When hovering the head, beak and tail point downwards, with the bird almost doubling on itself. Female has only one, broken, collar compared to male's two. A rather common bird in the lowlands with a preference for large open bodies of water and marshes. Its diet is predominantly fish and crustaceans. It utters a sustained, chattering *chililip, chililip* in flight. Often in pairs.

(Little) Green Bee-eater *Merops orientalis* 25 cm (inc. tail)

The constant twittering of Green Bee-eaters is a part of the background music of open spaces in the low country dry zone. This species has a marked preference for low perches and seems to engage in a vertical partitioning of air space with Chestnut-headed Bee-eater (*Merops leschenaulti*) having the middle space and Blue-tailed Bee-eater (*Merops philippinus*) the upper air space. Sri Lankan race has blue throat with juvenile showing green. Green Bee-eater is reminiscent of Blue-tailed with its chestnut underwings, central tail feathers and dark line through eye continuous with the dark beak. However, it is much smaller and has blue throat, unlike yellow and brown of Blue-tailed. It utters a repeated short trill *tirri, tirri, tirri*.

Blue-tailed Bee-eater *Merops philippinus* 30 cm (inc. tail)

A common migrant that disperses throughout the country. Small parties will even take up residence in the tall trees in Colombo. The throat colour and lack of a black line across neck distinguish it from the other bee-eaters. It has a little yellow and a lot of brown on the throat, the reverse of Chestnut-headed Bee-eater (*Merops leschenaulti*). The long central tail feathers are prominent. A conspicuous migrant, especially on arrival, as small flocks call when they fly overhead: a repeated, soft but far-carrying trill *tirrip, tirrip, tirrip*. It takes up position on a high perch from which it sallies after aerial insects, returning to its perch in flycatcher fashion.

86

European Bee-eater *Merops apiaster* 28 cm (inc. tail)

Namal Kamalgoda

A large, colourful bee-eater, somewhat similar to Chestnut-headed Bee-eater (*Merops leschenaulti*) in appearance, but larger. Its forehead is white, head to upper-back chestnut, scapulars golden-yellow; throat yellow and rest of the underparts blue. It has a short central tail projection. A recently recorded rare winter migrant but a flock now annually visits Ruhuna National Park. The call is a far-carrying trill *prrit, prrit*. It occurs with flocks of other bee-eaters, particularly Blue-tailed Bee-eater (*Merops philippinus*).

Chestnut-headed Bee-eater *Merops leschenaulti* 21 cm

A common resident in the lowlands and mid hills provided there are wooded areas. The chestnut head and upper back and lack of central tail projection distinguish it from other bee-eaters, but take care not to overlook European Bee-eater (*Merops apiaster*), a scarce migrant which has superficially similar chestnut and green upperparts. However, European is easily told apart by its sky-blue underparts sharply delineated by a black line from the lemon-yellow throat. It also has a lot of chestnut on the wings unlike Chestnut-headed Bee-eater. The call is a shrill *trillip, trillip*.

T.S.U. de Zylva

87

Indian Roller *Coracias benghalensis* 32–34 cm

T.S.U. de Zylva

An rather dull bird when perched, in flight the wings are vividly banded light and dark blue. It is found throughout the lowlands upto the mid hills, it is not shy of man and pairs will often frequent cricket pitches in Colombo. It is commoner in the dry zone where it will sit perched on a dead tree ready to pounce on an unsuspecting insect on the ground or intercept one in the air. The commonest call is a short harsh *chak*, repeated at intervals.

Dollarbird (Asian Broad-billed Roller)
Eurystomus orientalis 28–31 cm

T.S.U. de Zylva

(Endangered). This species was formerly considered very rare in the island, and thought to be extinct during the first half of the 20th century. It is now known to be widespread except in the higher hills and the driest areas. It favours 'edge habitats' of forests, staying perched on bare trees looking out for its insect prey, which it catches in flight. It is regularly seen in Sinharaja and Kitulgala, at clearings in the forest. Overall a dark bird with a peacock-blue sheen. Bill orange-red. In flight shows whitish 'dollars' on the underwings. The call is a harsh *chack, chack*.

Common Hoopoe *Upupa epops* 28–32 cm

An uncommon bird of well-wooded forests in the low country dry zone. Despite its preference for wooded regions, it forages on open spaces for insects and larvae. It will visit orchards and village gardens and hunt for insects by digging. It has an orange-brown head and underparts with zebra style black and white barring on the wings and tail. Its repeated soft *oopoop-oop* song gives the bird its name.

* Sri Lanka Grey Hornbill *Ocyceros gingalensis* 59 cm

Endemic. Locally common species widely distributed throughout lowlands and lower hills. Frequently found in disturbed forests and at forest fringes (especially in wet zone), and adjoining well-wooded gardens. However, it is scarce in the core of the wet zone evergreen forests. Usually found in pairs or small flocks, although large gatherings may be seen on fruiting trees. It utters a goat-like call *kaaaa*; the song is a rapid, rising, nasal, far-carrying *kak-kak-kak-kak*. Usually found in pairs, female is distinguished by upper mandible having a yellowish patch against otherwise dark bill. Male in contrast has yellow bill with a dark patch intruding at the base. Both sexes lack a casque. Overall, is uniform grey, paler on underparts with chestnut on vent.

Malabar Pied Hornbill *Anthracoceros coronatus* 92 cm

These striking birds, with their contrasting black and white plumage and casqued bills, are unmistakable. Usually found in small flocks that can be easily located by their raucous yelping call *kak-kak-kak-kak-kaak-kak* that fluctuates in volume. A calling single bird can give the impression of the presence of a small flock. The sexes are easily told apart. Female lacks the black mark at rear end of the upper mandible, and also has a pale ring around eye that contrasts with black face. The birds prefer tall forests in the dry lowlands. They form large flocks for feeding and roosting.

T.S.U. de Zylva

Brown-headed Barbet *Megalaima zeylanica* 25–27 cm

A common resident throughout the island up to the mid-hills. A garden bird readily found even in heavily built up areas where there is tree cover. It will visit bird tables if fruits are provided. The birds excavate a nesting burrow, usually high up on an old exposed branch or tree trunk, out of reach of most predators. Its song is one of the most familiar of bird sounds: an unmistakable *ku-krroo, ku-krroo*, repeated and sometimes starting with a rattling 'run-up'. Easily distinguished from other barbets by its size, streaked brown head and bare yellow skin around the eye.

T.S.U. de Zylva

★ Yellow-fronted Barbet *Megalaima flavifrons* 21–22 cm

Gehan de Silva Wijeyeratne

(Vulnerable). Endemic. Common in well-wooded areas in wet lowlands to mid hills. Also common in the foothills to mid hills on the drier, eastern side of the mountains. Its pleasing, far-carrying calls, heard throughout the day, are the most characteristic sound of all the forested areas of the wet zone lowlands and adjacent hills: a repeated *ku-ki-yuk, ku-ki-yuk* with the middle syllable higher in pitch, and a rapid repeated *kwoik, kwoik* with a rattling prelude. The second-largest barbet in the island, it is unmistakable with its blue face and yellow forehead. It frequents tall trees, but descends to lower trees especially when these are in fruit.

★ Ceylon Small Barbet
Megalaima rubricapilla 16–17 cm

T.S.U. de Zylva

Endemic. A small, beautiful barbet common throughout lowlands to the mid hills. The only endemic regularly seen in major cities. Easily overlooked due to its small size and colour; predominantly green with red forehead, blue lower face, orange throat and 'spectacles'. These features and uniform green underparts readily distinguish it from Coppersmith Barbet (*Megalaima haemacephala*) in areas where both are found. Lives in pairs but single birds often seen on tall trees, and flocks may be found on fruiting trees. Male has two songs, uttered from tall treetops: a slow repeated *pop, pop, pop* and a rapidly repeated *popo-popo-popo-pop* with a variable number of syllables.

91

Yellow-crowned Woodpecker (Yellow-fronted Pied Woodpecker) *Dendrocopos mahrattensis* 17–19 cm

Ismeth Raheem

Found in parklands of the dry lowlands, often in pairs working their way around the trees. The black upperparts, heavily spotted with white, are superficially similar to smaller Brown-capped Pygmy Woodpecker (*Dendrocopos nanus*). The yellow forehead, pale face without an eye stripe and larger size differentiate it. Sexes similar except that female lacks red on the hind crown and nape, instead having an all yellow crown.

Rufous Woodpecker *Celeus brachyurus* 24–25 cm

T.S.U. de Zylva

(Low risk). An unmistakable woodpecker due to its rufous coloration with black barring. Male has small crimson patch below eye which is only visible at close range. Juvenile similar to adults. Found in forests, it has an unusual nesting habit of excavating a nest hole in the fairly solid nests of tree-dwelling ants. Lives in pairs and usually feed separately from each other, keeping in contact by uttering a loud sharp three syllable call *queep-queep-queep* from time to time. An uncommon resident distributed in the lowlands and up to the mid hills.

Lesser Yellownape (Lesser Yellow-naped Woodpecker)
Picus chlorolophus 24–26 cm

This bird is rather common but sometimes thought to be rare on account of its unobtrusive behaviour. It is confined to lowlands and lower hills of the wet zone. It is not unusual to find a mixed species feeding flock accompanied by a pair of these birds. It can be seen visiting gardens with large trees. The only species it is likely to be confused with is scarcer Streak-throated Woodpecker (*Picus xanthopygaeus*). The latter lacks yellow nape, is larger, has scaling and not spots on the underparts and has a yellow and not green rump. The call is a loud sharp long-drawn single-note *keeer*.

Streak-throated Woodpecker (Small Scaly-bellied Woodpecker) *Picus xanthopygaeus* 28–30 cm

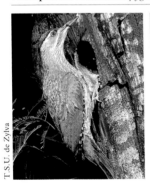

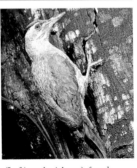

(Left) *male;* (above) *female*

(Vulnerable). A medium-sized green woodpecker which may spend a long time feeding on the ground, unlike other woodpeckers. Female lacks red on crown present in male. This bird differs from similar Lesser Yellownape (*Picus chlorolophus*) by having pale green upperparts, whitish underparts with fine scaly markings, and yellow rump. It lives in pairs, but when mates are wide apart they keep in contact by uttering sharp *queep* calls. An uncommon resident with a small range from the mid hills of drier eastern side of mountains down to grasslands of foothills and adjoining lowlands.

93

Black-rumped Flameback (Red-backed Woodpecker)
Dinopium benghalense psarodes 26–29 cm

Probably the most familiar woodpecker in Sri Lanka. Its song, a rattling scream *ki-ki-ki-ki-ki-…kikikik* which first rises, then falls in pitch and accelerates, gives away its presence although it is otherwise unobtrusive and many city dwellers are unaware that this striking bird is found in residential areas. Sometimes also utters a slow *ki-ki* note. The red back and black and white on head and neck is distinctive, and can only be confused with Greater Flameback (*Chrysocolaptes lucidus*). The latter has an ivory-coloured, not dark, beak and a white 'island' on the chin. Female has black on forecrown rather than red. In the dry lowlands northwards of North Central province, a golden-backed race of this woodpecker occurs.

T.S.U. de Zylva

White-naped Woodpecker (Black-backed Yellow Woodpecker) *Chrysocolaptes festivus* 29 cm

(Vulnerable). A beautifully-coloured, large woodpecker which is unmistakable due to its tri-coloured upperparts in black, white and yellow. Male has red crown and crest but those of the female are yellow. It lives in pairs, but the pair may feed separately quite a distance apart. Prefers wooded habitats with large trees, including coconut groves. It utters a repeated, high-pitched trill *tirrip, tirrip* which seems very weak for the size of the bird. It is an uncommon resident in the dry lowlands and some adjoining wet areas. Recent records have been mostly from the south-east and the Chilaw, Kurunegala and Gampaha districts.

Eric Lott

94

Indian Pitta *Pitta brachyura* 19 cm

T.S.U. de Zylva

Sri Lanka has a reputation for being one of the best places to see this exquisite bird. A migrant that disperses throughout the island right up to the highlands. It can be encountered in forest, village gardens and town parks. Like many birds with striking plumage, evolution has not endowed it with a musical call or song. Its territorial song is a distinctive loud *queek-quiyo* in which the first syllable is higher. The scold notes are a harsh *queeeya* and a clearer *keeee*. It is a shy ground dweller, hopping about quietly in the undergrowth.

Rufous-winged Bushlark *Mirafra assamica* 15 cm

T.S.U. de Zylva

A common bird in the dry parklands. Every tree stump seems to have a singing male in the breeding season which often 'song flights' into the air before parachuting down. From the Pipits and Oriental Skylark (*Alauda gulgula*) it can be distinguished by stockier build, rufous wing patch and lack of pale edges to tail. Often seen walking on roads in the national parks, flying to a nearby bush when the vehicle approaches close. The song is a soft, very high-pitched, cicada-like *tseet-seet-seet-seet*.

Oriental Skylark (Indian Skylark) *Alauda gulgula* 16 cm

T.S.U. de Zylva

The sustained song of the male is a recital of sweet, musical-sounding phrases, sung from high in the air when the bird is a mere speck. This bird may be confused with Rufous-winged Bushlark (*Mirafra assamica*) but the latter is stockier, browner, shorter necked and usually shows a rufous wing patch. Pipits have a slimmer, more upright build and more 'under carriage' with the tibia showing and white edges to tail, whereas those of Oriental Skylark are buff. Uncommon resident found in open parkland in dry lowlands and drier part of hills.

Sand Martin *Riparia riparia* 13 cm

Tim Loseby

A small swallow with rather pale brown upperparts and whitish underparts. It has a brown band across the breast and a short tail with 'notched' end. It is a scarce but regular winter migrant mainly to the southeast coastal areas and usually associates with flocks of Barn Swallows (*Hirundo rustica*). In Sri Lanka it is not found in the large flocks typical in their breeding grounds. Dusky Crag Martin (*Hirundo concolor*) has also been recorded and is similar to Sand Martin in shape but is overall a dark brown with pale spots on tail as in swallows.

Barn Swallow (Common Swallow) *Hirundo rustica* 18 cm

T.S.U. de Zylva

A common migrant found throughout the island. It is abundant in the lowlands. Huge numbers roost on electric wires along the main roads in and around Ratnapura. During the daytime flocks rest on electric wires or on grass plains. The long tail streamers, dark blue upperparts and pale underparts distinguish this bird. Three migrant races are found. The commonest is *gutturalis* which has pale underparts with an incomplete black collar. Less common is *rustica* with pale underparts and a complete black collar. A rarity is *tytleri* with chestnut underparts, and an incomplete black collar.

Pacific Swallow (Hill Swallow)
Hirundo tahitica domicola 13 cm

Eric Lott

(Endangered). An uncommon resident confined to the hills. It can be distinguished from migrant Barn Swallow (*Hirundo rustica*) by grey underparts, lack of breast band and 'notched' tail without streamers. Visitors to the highlands are likely to see this bird perched on roadside telephone wires. Its preference for the hills explains its local name of Hill Swallow. It is rarely seen in large flocks like the migrant Barn Swallow.

97

Red-rumped Swallow (Ceylon Swallow) *Hirundo daurica hyperythra* 17–19 cm

T.S.U. de Zylva

Three races occur in Sri Lanka. The common local race, *hyperythra*, has red underparts and rump. *Nipalensis* is a vagrant distinguished by pale underparts and bold streaking. *Erythropygia* is a scarce migrant sometimes in flocks of varying numbers and is similar to *nipalensis* but with finer streaking. The local race is found throughout the lowlands and ascends the lower hills. It is easily distinguished from migrant Barn Swallow (*Hirundo rustica*) by the conspicuous red rump and chunkier build. Occurs in a range of habitats, from lightly forested valleys to paddy fields. Usually in pairs, sometimes may be seen in small flocks.

Paddyfield Pipit (Indian Pipit) *Anthus rufulus* 15–16 cm

T.S.U. de Zylva

A small brown ground bird of open grass and bare ground. The brown feathers of upperparts have dark centres. Underparts whitish with brownish tinge, which become a little darker on flanks. Some dark streaks on breast, which reduce with wear. Fairly erect posture and jerky gait. Often calls in flight; the call is *chip, chip*, plus sometimes *chip, chi-chi-chip*, usually uttered while flying. The song is *chi-chi-chi-chi*, higher-pitched than the call, and uttered in display flight during the breeding season. Resident throughout the island, more abundant in the dry zone and hills. Beware similar but larger Richard's Pipit (*Anthus richardi*), which is a scarce winter visitor.

98

Blyth's Pipit *Anthus godlewskii* 17 cm

Scarce but regular migrant to lowlands of Sri Lanka, especially to Uda Walawe National Park. Similar to common Paddyfield Pipit (*Anthus rufulus*) from which distinguished by dark streaking on paler upperparts. Overall, it is a paler bird with obvious pale face, especially around lores. Adult has diagnostic dark square-ish centres to the median coverts as opposed to triangular centres in Paddyfield Pipit. It is also a little larger but this is not readily apparent as they are not usually seen in mixed flocks. Tends to walk in a crouched fashion that lends it a more horizontal posture. The flight note is another reliable diagnostic feature, a short *pcheeo*. Prefers tussocky, grassy habitats and often found singly.

Gehan De Silva Wijeyeratne

Forest Wagtail *Dendronanthus indicus* 17–18 cm

T.S.U. de Zylva

A common migrant from north-east Asia, it occurs throughout the island but is most likely to be encountered in the forests of the dry zone. It usually occurs in pairs with both sexes similar. Unlike wagtails, wags tail from side to side, and may be seen frequently perching on trees. Its smart but camouflaged plumage patterned in brown and white would make it hard to see were it not for its movements as it forages on the forest floor. The call is a high-pitched, repeated, metallic *pink*. Large numbers gather at evening roosts.

Yellow Wagtail *Motacilla flava* 18 cm

T.S.U. de Zylva

A winter migrant, mainly to the dry lowlands. Frequents open grass patches near water. In all plumages, adults distinguished from other wagtails by olive upper-back. Several races have been recorded; the common race *thunbergi* (Grey-headed Yellow Wagtail) has dark grey head and bright yellow underparts in breeding plumage. In non-breeding plumage, it has greyish-brown head, sometimes with a pale eyebrow, and less yellow underparts. Young birds have brown upperparts and whitish underparts. Call, which is uttered in flight, is a sharp *tsreep*, sometimes repeated.

Grey Wagtail *Motacilla cinerea* 19 cm

T.S.U. de Zylva

Often seen searching for insects in damp areas. Its call draws attention as it alights on a roof or wall, before settling on the ground. Longer tail and grey on head, neck and mantle distinguish it from Yellow Wagtail (*Motacilla flava*) which also has yellow on underparts. In breeding plumage, the white throat turns black forming a white malar stripe, joining the white eye line at the bill base, forming a 'V'. Its call is a *tchi-chip, tchi-chip*, plus sometimes *tchi-chi-chip*, usually uttered in flight.

Ceylon Woodshrike *Tephrodornis pondicerianus* 16 cm

Endemic. An arboreal, shrike-like, grey-coloured bird. Fairly common in the dry zone. Female is a little duller and browner than the male. Both have a blackish stripe across the eye like that in the true shrikes. Lives in pairs. The calls are a five-to-seven syllabled *chee-chee-chee-...* with the first syllables hurried, and the rest descending and a loud *twee* sound often in the same pattern. In dry zone ascends up to the mid hills; scarcer and local throughout the wet zone.

Gehan de Silva Wijeyeratne

Black-headed Cuckooshrike *Coracina melanoptera* 19 cm

Pathmanath Samaraweera

A rather common bird in well-wooded areas of the dry lowlands. Usually seen in pairs. Male has black head and unmarked underparts whereas female has grey head and is barred on underparts. Both sexes have white tips on the outer tail feathers which are noticeable in flight. Female differs from Large Cuckooshrike (*Coracina macei*) by smaller size and build. The birds are quite discreet as they move about in the canopy and can be easily overlooked. The song is a loud, clear, sweet *twit-twit-twee-twee-twee-twee*.

101

Scarlet Minivet (Orange Minivet) *Pericrocotus flammeus* 20 cm

T.S.U. de Zylva

Male is unmistakable, being a combination of scarlet and black. Female has scarlet replaced with yellow and black with grey. Immature male similar to female with some orange patches on yellow. Can be confused with Small Minivet (*Pericrocotus cinnamomeus*), but the male of latter has more grey on head and female has white on the belly. Despite the vivid colours, minivets are excellently camouflaged in the forest canopy, where the vivid patches of colour serve to break up the outline of the bird. The small, active flocks maintain a constant medley of contact calls as they forage. They utter a high-pitched sweet *twee-twee, twititi-twit-twitit*, sometimes extended, when flying from one tree to another. In mixed species flocks this species combs the upper and middle layers.

Small Minivet (Little Minivet)
Pericrocotus cinnamomeus 15–16 cm

T.S.U. de Zylva

Small Minivets keep to the tops of tall trees. Their patchy colouration of sober greys with contrasting orange blends in with the canopy. It is the commoner of the two minivet species and tends to travel in small flocks, often in a 'follow my leader' procession. In a flock they utter a soft, very high-pitched *tweet, twee-twee-tweet* while flying between trees. It is found in village garden habitats wherever good stands of tall trees are found. In good forests, Little Minivets join feeding flocks comprising several species.

(Top) *female;* (bottom) *male*

Bar-winged Flycatcher-shrike (Pied Flycatcher-shrike)
Hemipus picatus leggei 14 cm

Rukshan Jayawardene

The Sri Lankan race is endemic with both sexes similar. A small bird with strongly contrasting black and white plumage. It moves in small flocks. It is found throughout the island and commonest where good stands of forest are available. The birds are often found in mixed feeding flocks. It prefers the canopy and may escape detection unless given away but its contact calls. The call is *chiri-chiri-wit, chiri-chiri-wit, chirity, chirity*.

* Black-crested Bulbul (Black-capped Bulbul)
Pycnonotus melanicterus 18 cm

T.S.U. de Zylva

(Low risk). Endemic. A fairly common species in forests and nearby gardens in wet lowlands to the lower hills. It is also found in the dry zone forests of the North Central Province (e.g. Giritale), intermediate forests in the South, tall forests and riverine forests in Udawalawe National Park and Yala National Park (Blocks 1 & 3). An easy bird to see as it frequents low trees and bushes in edge habitats. Usually seen in pairs but sometimes seen in small flocks. Often hovers briefly like a sunbird as it catches insects. In flight, the white tip to tail is prominent. It has soft whistling songs, some of them with a rather mournful quality and the call is a rapid *pit-pit-pipit*.

103

Red-vented Bulbul *Pycnonotus cafer* 20 cm

Gehan De Silva Wijeyeratne

A familiar garden bird encountered in villages and town. Common in gardens even in densely populated cities. Distinguished by its dark crest, red vent and perky habits. Its habit of nesting in light bulb shades and other positions inconvenient to householders is treated with much tolerance. Very vocal; many sounds have a loud, lively and pleasant quality. The usual call-note is *tchreek* but also has harsh, scolding notes.

* Yellow-eared Bulbul *Pycnonotus penicillatus* 19 cm

T.S.U. de Zylva

(Endangered). Endemic. A common species in forests and gardens of the higher hills. An unmistakable bird with its prominent yellow ear-tufts. Found in pairs or in small flocks. Easily seen in bushes and low trees. Regularly seen in bird waves in the hills. Tangamalai Sanctuary in Haputale, Hakgala Botanical Gardens, wooded sites in Nuwara Eliya and Horton Plains National Park are good places to see this species. The flight call, uttered often while moving from bush to bush, is a loud, sweet, rather quick *weet, wit-wit, wit-wit*.

White-browed Bulbul *Pycnonotus luteolus* 20 cm

Pathmanath Samaraweera

A rather shy bird occurring in gardens and forest. It is found mainly in the lowlands, ascends to mid hills and is most abundant in dry areas. Identified by its white supercilium, drab colouration and yellow vent, which is not always seen. The characteristic call, 'a loud rattle of sweetish notes', is a familiar sound of the dry-zone forests.

Yellow-browed Bulbul *Iole indica* 20 cm

T.S.U. de Zylva

More frequent in wet zone forests ascending to the mid hills. Identified by its black eye in a yellow face and its many whistling calls: a pure-toned *twee-twee* and other sweet, loud sounds. Small flocks or pairs forage in the middle levels for invertebrates. Its overall yellow colour and calls will distinguish it from Black-crested Bulbul (*Pycnonotus melanicterus*) which occurs in the same habitat.

105

Square-tailed Black Bulbul *Hypsipetes ganeesa* 24–25 cm

Gehan de Silva Wijeyeratne

Because of its strongly vocal habits possibly the most conspicuous bird in good wet zone and hill forests. Blackish overall except for the red beak and legs. It makes various raucous calls, the commonest being a loud *tchrek, tchreeek*. Calls conspicuously from an exposed branch high in the canopy. A rather common bird in the hills, found even in severely degraded forests which are mixed with plantations. Its occurrence in the dry zone is local and tends to be restricted to wetter forest patches.

Jerdon's Leafbird
Chloropsis jerdoni 19 cm

T.S.U. de Zylva

Leaf-green, and like all leafbirds excellently camouflaged. This coupled with its preference for the canopy means it is overlooked, and regularly visits suburban gardens. Male distinguished from Gold-fronted Leafbird (*Chloropsis aurifrons*) by absence of orange-yellow forehead, throat patch not extending back further than the eye, and distinct yellowish border to throat patch. Female has blue throat patch which is lacking in female Gold-fronted. Utters a sustained variety of loud whistling and rather harsh notes. It is a fine mimic of other bird species.

Golden-fronted Leafbird (Gold-fronted Chloropsis)
Chloropsis aurifrons 19 cm

Gehan de Silva Wijeyeratne

Frequents the canopy, so difficult to see. Found throughout the island, except higher hills, wherever tree cover is available. It is less common than the other leafbird. Male easily identified by golden forehead. Female has reduced markings. Utters a range of clear, far-carrying whistling notes. The male's song is usually delivered from a treetop or other vantage point. It mimics other bird species.

Common Iora *Aegithina tiphia* 14 cm

Rukshan Jayawardane

Common in village gardens and forests, found throughout the lowlands and mid hills, frequenting the mid level and canopy. It is very vocal, but can be difficult to see. Male unmistakable with blue-black upperparts and yellow underparts. Female dull yellow with green tinge on upperparts and two white wingbars. Usually in pairs. The iora has a variety of sweet whistles, some long-drawn, one a drowsy-sounding *weeeeee-cho* rising in pitch and dropping suddenly. It also utters a soft long-drawn descending rattle. Two of its calls sometimes mistaken to be the 'Pretty Dear' song of the Brown-capped Babbler (*Pellorneum fuscocapillum*).

T.S.U. de Zylva

(Top) *male;* (below) *female*

Indian Blue Robin (Indian Blue Chat) *Luscinia brunnea* 14 cm

T.S.U. de Zylva

A skulking ground bird. Male is striking with blue upperparts, chestnut-orange underparts and white supercilium. Female has brown upperparts and pale purple-buff underparts. Female can be confused with Brown-capped Babbler (*Pellorneum fuscocapillum*) but the latter is larger and has a distinct dark cap. Indian Blue Robin has a habit of rhythmically wagging its tail up and down unlike Brown-capped Babbler. A winter migrant throughout the island, solitary birds inhabiting the undergrowth. Song is a distinctive high-pitched *keek, keek, keekiri-keekiri*. The alarm call is a repeated *tet, tet*.

Oriental Magpie Robin *Copsychus saularis* 19–21 cm

Namal Kamalgoda

A strong contender for the most musical bird in Sri Lanka, rivalled perhaps only by White-rumped Shama (*Copysychus malabaricus*). A familiar garden bird, often seen singing with great gusto. Its repertoire is varied and it intersperses long melancholy passages with rapid, musical sequences. The scold note is a harsh screech. Female has greyish-black upperparts and greyish breast. The birds feed mainly on ground-dwelling invertebrates.

108

White-rumped Shama *Copsychus malabaricus* 26 cm

A long-tailed bird of forest and dense scrub. A ventriloqual song-ster. Black upperparts, deep orange underparts, long tail dark above and white below, and a conspicuous white rump which is obvious in flight. Female differs by the tail being a little shorter. Rich, melodious song, including passages with a 'rattling' quali-ty. Song more fluty than that of Oriental Magpie Robin (*Copsy-chus saularis*).

Pied Bush-Chat *Saxicola caprata* 14 cm

(Left) *male;* (above) *female*

(Endangered). A highland species, often seen perched on low bushs or telephone wires. The male is all black with white rump, upper and undertail coverts. The distinct white diagonal wingbar is absent in the female. Female dull brown with rufous uppertail-coverts and dirty-white undertail-coverts. The call is a rather soft, high-pitched, repeated *cleew, cleew*. The song is a repeated *chi-chiu-chi-chee*, each phrase rising at the end.

Indian Robin *Saxicoloides fulicatus* 16–19 cm

Gehan de Silva Wijeyeratne

Resembles a smaller version of Oriental Magpie-Robin (*Copsychus saularis*) in shape and general habits, but the male is entirely black with rufous undertail coverts and the female is dark brown with rufous undertail coverts. Male shows a white patch on the wings in flight. The usual call is a sibilant high-pitched *chi-chee, chi-chee* the *chee* rising, but it makes other calls of four to seven notes of the same tone. It also has a fairly short but fine song. Common resident garden bird in the dry lowlands and fairly common up to the mid hills, but rare and scattered in the wet zone.

* Ceylon Whistling-thrush *Myophoneus blighi* 20–21 cm

Gehan de Silva Wijeyeratne

Ceylon Whistling-thrush male (left) and female (right)

(Endangered). Endemic. This species has one of the most restricted ranges of Sri Lankan birds. Confined to montane forests, mainly Horton Plains National Park, Peak Wilderness Sanctuary area and Knuckles Wilderness Area. A rather rare and elusive forest species inhabiting dense undergrowth by streams, ponds and waterholes in higher hills. Most active at dawn and dusk. Male black with glossy blue shoulder patch, usually hidden. Female brown overall but with the blue patch. Call is a sharp, very high-pitched whistle *sreee...*

Pied Thrush (Pied Ground Thrush) *Zoothera wardii* 22 cm

T.S.U. de Zylva

The black and white male is the most attractively patterned of the Sri Lankan thrushes. The female is similarly patterned to male but brown with pale eye-brow, pale spots on upperparts, and dark markings on pale underparts. A shy bird usually feeding under bushes and in adjoining ditches. When not feeding, usually rests in thick foliage of tall trees. Often found in well-covered areas near human habitation. Its call is a short very soft and high-pitched *sree*. Occasionally wintering males sing a rather soft, high-pitched, sweet song from the tree-tops. An uncommon winter migrant from northern India to the mid hills and higher altitudes. Regular at Victoria Park, Nuwara Eliya.

Orange-headed Thrush (Orange-headed Ground Thrush)
Zoothera citrina 21–23 cm

T.S.U. de Zylva

A stunningly-coloured migrant from northern India. Female differs from male in having olive upper back, blue-grey in male, otherwise resembles male. A rare but regular winter visitor to the lowlands and lower hills. Solitary birds take up territory mostly close to human settlement. This can be home gardens in towns, villages or in forests. Male has a sweet, varied rather soft song which is somewhat reminiscent of sub-songs of Oriental Magpie-Robin (*Copsychus saularis*). Usually starts singing on and off from February, before it finally leaves around April.

111

* **Spot-winged Thrush** *Zoothera spiloptera* 21 cm

T.S.U. de Zylva

(Vulnerable). Endemic. Mainly a ground-dwelling species, fairly common in forests and adjoining plantations, and gardens in the lowlands, to the hills of wet zone. Scarce and locally distributed in riverine forests in dry zone. The melodious whistling song of this shy thrush is often heard without the bird being seen. It may be possible to locate this species feeding on forest trails in the mornings and evenings. Its calls are tuneful, human-sounding whistles, commonly concluded with a rapid, rising three or four note *whew-whew...* Kitulgala and Sinharaja are good sites for this species. Other sites where one may look for it include Bodhinagala, Gilimale, Surrey Estate, Tangamalai Sanctuary, the upper forest section of Hakgala Botanical Gardens and Horton Plains.

Scaly Thrush *Zoothera dauma imbricata* 24 cm

T.S.U. de Zylva

(Endangered). A large, secretive, attractively-patterned ground thrush. The golden-buff scaly pattern and stocky shape distinguish it from other thrushes and immatures of similar birds, which show pale spots or scaly pattern. Inhabits undergrowth of thick wet forests but may appear in the adjoining open patches, usually in the early morning. An uncommon bird confined to the forests in the lower hills and higher altitudes in the wet zone. It has a rather soft, plain whistle, often repeated and sung at dawn. It also has a short high-pitched alarm call which may be uttered any time of the day.

112

Indian Blackbird *Turdus simillimus kinnisii* 25 cm

Gehan de Silva Wijeyeratne

(Endangered). A typical upland bird in Sri Lanka restricted to the higher mountains. In highland towns like Nuwara Eliya it can be seen in parks and gardens. This shy bird is often encountered in the remaining montane forests of the Horton Plains National Park. The Sri Lankan race was considered a 'good' species in the 19th century and then downgraded to a sub-species. The bright orange bill and dull orange legs make it noticeably different from Eurasian Blackbird seen in Europe.

★ Ceylon Bush-warbler (Ceylon Warbler)
Elaphrornis palliseri 15–16 cm

T.S.U. de Zylva

(Endangered). Endemic. A rather common but very secretive species in the high mountain undergrowth and scrub. Lives in pairs and often located by its characteristic high-pitched contact calls, a short *quich* and a squirrel-like *chink*. However, similar calls, though lower in pitch, are issued by Common Tailorbird (*Orthotomus sutorius*), found in the same habitat. The Bush Warbler is often found in bird waves. Male has red and female pale buff irides. The bushy area by the stream below the Hakgala main road, the bushy areas in the upper and lower sections of Hakgala Botanical Gardens, Galway's Land Sanctuary in Nuwara Eliya and the forest in Horton Plains are good sites.

113

Zitting Cisticola
Cisticola juncidis 10 cm

One of the most widespread birds on the island, occurring from the lowlands to the highland plateau of the Horton Plains National Park. It is a small, active bird inhabiting paddy fields, marshlands and grasslands, and frequently draws attention to itself as it launches into the air, giving its 'zitting' call in weak display flight. Its call, heavy streaking on crown and mantle, and the fan-shaped tail makes identification easy. Two races: wet zone and dry zone.

Gehan de Silva Wijeyeratne

Plain Prinia *Prinia inornata* 13 cm

T.S.U. de Zylva

A common bird in the lowlands, less so in the hills. Found even within cities in unused grassland plots. The distinct white supercilium separates it from other prinias. Similar Jungle Prinia (*Prinia sylvatica*) has indistinct half supercilium and buffy underparts compared to off-white underparts of Plain Prinia. An active bird that flits around in tall grass. Best seen when it pauses to sing from an exposed perch. The most frequently heard song is a rapid *clik-clik-clik*. Other vocalisations include sharp churring sounds.

114

Ashy Prinia *Prinia socialis brevicauda* 12 cm

Eric Lott

Found throughout the island, commoner in dry zone and encountered in grass, shrubs and marshland. The ashy upper-parts and buff underparts separate this species from other prinias. Not quite as abundant as Plain Prinia (*Prinia inornata*). Female is little browner with a slight whitish half supercilium. It utters a *chwih, chwih* somewhat like the call of Common Tailorbird (*Orthotomus sutorius*), a rapid *chi-chi-chip, chi-chi-chip* and a song *chilip, chilip...* It has a distinctive scolding note, a peevish, descending *tee, tee, tee...*

Common Tailorbird *Orthotomus sutorius* 12–14 cm

One of the commonest garden birds, widely distributed throughout the island. It has a loud call quite out of proportion to its size. The chestnut cap, greenish body and upwardly cocked tail make it easy to identify. It spends most of it time threading its way through the shrub layer in search of invertebrates. Female has shorter tail. She 'sews' edges of large leaves together to form the nest. The call is a familiar *chuwit, chuwit*, a *chiyok, chiyok*, and a high-pitched *pit-pit-pit-pit*. Two endemic races: *sutorius* to 1,500 m, *fernandonis* in higher hills.

T.S.U. de Zylva

Clamorous Reed Warbler *Acrocephalus stentoreus* 18–19 cm

Chandima Kahandawala

A large, mainly brown warbler which lives in reed clumps of ponds, lakes, tanks and marshlands in the dry lowlands. It is the largest of the Sri Lankan warblers. Not difficult to recognise due to its larger size – about the size of a House Sparrow (*Passer domesticus*), shape and simple brown and whitish colour pattern. A shy bird, its loud rattling song is more often heard than it is seen. Gives a short hard *tak* call. It is a rather common resident at suitable habitats in the dry zone, only occasionally found in the wet zone.

Tickell's Blue Flycatcher *Cyornis tickelliae* 14–15 cm

T.S.U. de Zylva

A fairly common forest resident from the wet lowlands to the mid hills but is also found in suitable forests in the dry zone. The female is duller with a lighter orange throat and breast unlike those of the male's which are rich orange. Both sexes lack the blue throat of the rare male Blue-throated Flycatcher (*Cyornis rubeculoides*). The melodious jingling song is commonly heard in forest, but the bird can at times be difficult to see. Also utters a sharp *kik, kik* call. It is sometimes found in well-wooded gardens. Not very shy, and can be inquisitive towards humans.

116

*Dull-blue Flycatcher (Dusky-blue Flycatcher)
Eumyias sordida 15 cm

T.S.U. de Zylva

(Endangered). Endemic. A dusky-blue bird with prominent light-blue forehead. Rather common in forests and well-wooded gardens in higher hills. Several may be seen feeding separately in close vicinity. It has a distinctive, soft, sweet and somewhat sad-sounding song, rising in pitch towards the end, and a similar but more even-pitched song. Regularly found in bird waves. Hakgala, Galway's Land Sanctuary and Victoria Park in Nuwara Eliya, Horton Plains and Knuckles are good places to see it.

Brown-breasted Flycatcher (Layard's Flycatcher)
Muscicapa muttui 14–15 cm

T.S.U. de Zylva

A small, predominantly brown flycatcher found fairly close to the ground in well-wooded areas. It has rich brown upperparts and distinctly brownish breast and flanks. A white patch around the eye, especially in front and behind, is very conspicuous, and it has a whitish moustachial stripe and brown sub-moustachial. Its legs and feet are pale, being yellowish-pink. The above features help to distinguish this species from the similar Asian Brown Flycatcher (*Muscicapa dauurica*). A solitary, mainly silent species, but occasionally gives a long, soft, high-pitched, warbling song from a low branch and a rather long-drawn, very high-pitched *eee* call when chasing a rival. Rather common winter migrant mainly to the wooded areas of the wet zone up to the mid hills.

Asian Brown Flycatcher (Brown Flycatcher)
Muscicapa dauurica 13 cm

Superficially similar to migrant Brown-breasted Flycatcher (*Muscicapa muttui*), but less richly coloured with more grey and has dark legs. It is less selective in its choice of habitat and can turn up anywhere. It seems partial to gardens and can be found even in densely populated cities as long as there are plenty of mature trees. Usually quite vocal. The calls are a somewhat loud *chik, chi-chi-chik, chi-chi-chi-chi-chik*, etc., and a high-pitched *treek*. A canopy species, often first detected by its regular calls. Flies in a loop, catches prey, and returns to perch.

Kashmir Flycatcher (Kashmir Red-breasted Flycatcher)
Ficedula subrubra 12–13 cm

A pretty little flycatcher found in higher hills during the northern winter. Male has greyish-brown upperparts; orange-rufous chin, throat and breast which merges onto belly and flanks; black streaks on each side of throat bordering chestnut colour; and rest of underparts is dusky white. Female similar to male except for paler rufous colour restricted to chin, throat and breast, and lacks black vertical lines on side of throat. Immature lacks rufous on breast. All have pale orangish colour on base of lower mandible. Usually solitary and found close to the ground, but will feed high up in trees. Call a rather high-pitched rapid rattle *ti-ti-ti-ti*. An uncommon winter migrant from north-west India; apparently the majority of the population winters in the hills of Sri Lanka.

118

Grey-headed Canary-flycatcher
Culicicapa ceylonensis 11.5–13 cm

Gehan de Silva Wijeyeratne

(Vulnerable). Found in uplands, being common in good stands of montane forest. Not shy and can be seen well in highland gardens and town parks provided good forest cover is not far away. The yellow body and grey head with a little crest readily identify it. Distinctive, pleasant four-note song *tee-tee, wee-tee*. Usually in pairs. Often joins mixed species feeding flocks.

White-browed Fantail
Rhipidura aureola 17–18 cm

T.S.U. de Zylva

The only species of fantail found on the island. Found in forest and village garden habitats from the lowlands to the mid hills. It is a common bird in tea plantations where pockets of trees persist. The unmistakable, melodious song is a loud whistling *ti-ti-tik, ti-tik-teek, twee-ti-tee-tweek*. Sometimes performs 'dancing' movements.

Black-naped Monarch (Black-naped Flycatcher)
Hypothymis azurea 16 cm

Its restless behaviour and frequent calls draw attention to this species. It has two calls, a strong, rasping *tchwee* with a 'ringing' quality, uttered often, and a rapid *pwit-pwit-pwit-pwit* of about nine syllables. Found in the lowlands to the mid hills, but most likely encountered in the wet forests. The behaviour and slender appearance easily distinguish it from the other blue flycatchers recorded on the island. A pair of these are a usual addition to the mixed feeding flocks in wet forests. Females and immatures are duller.

Asian Paradise-flycatcher (Ceylon Paradise Flycatcher)
Terpsiphone paradisi ceylonensis 20 cm (male: 30 cm tail)

Unmistakable, as it flits about in wooded habitats everywhere. This chestnut-coloured resident race breeds in the dry lowlands and lower hills, visiting other areas in the migrant season (northern winter). Female has shorter tail. Adult male distinguished by the long tail feathers that are longer than the body. The call, uttered often, is a harsh *tchree*, and the song, uttered occasionally, is a musical *twee-tee-twee-tyu*. Often flashes tail as it actively takes insects on the wing.

T.S.U. de Zylva

Asian Paradise-flycatcher (Indian Paradise-flycatcher)
Terpsiphone paradisi paradisi 20 cm (male: 30 cm tail)

The male is a beautiful sight with two white tail streamers, a white body and a black head. This is the migrant race which occupies much the same habitat as the local race. Immature males are chestnut like males of local race. After their third year they start moulting into white plumage. Females of this race also are as those of the local race. Calls of the two races are similar. Most likely seen in good forest in the lowlands, in both the dry and wet zones, but occasionally visits gardens.

T.S.U. de Zylva

---

* **Brown-capped Babbler** *Pellorneum fuscocapillum* 16 cm

T.S.U. de Zylva

Endemic. A fairly common and widespread bird except in the higher hills. Seldom seen due to its mainly ground-dwelling habits. Found in scrub jungle, primary forest and forest adjoining home gardens. Lives in pairs that maintain a territory. The song of the male is a loud, clear, three syllable whistle, often heard in the early part of the day: *tw'tee-tyow* with the *tee* higher in pitch and *tyow* descending. (This gives the bird the name 'Pretty Dear'.) It also has a musical scolding-song whose pitch descends in a 'zig-zag' manner.

121

Indian Scimitar Babbler
Pomatorhinus horsfieldii holdsworthi 22 cm

Found throughout the island ascending to the higher hills. Has a variety of mellow, bubbling calls. Male and female duet, the male calling *woop-oop-oopoop*, and in another song *yok, ko-ko*, and both are answered by the trilling sound of the female. Can be found in village gardens but is unlikely to be found in areas where good patches of forest are not nearby. Decurved yellow bill, prominent white supercilium and brown and white body make this an unmistakable bird. It lives in pairs.

T.S.U. de Zylva

Tawny-bellied Babbler (White-throated Babbler)
Dumetia hyperythra phillipsi 14 cm

T.S.U. de Zylva

An attractive little babbler, along with Dark-fronted, the smallest found in Sri Lanka. Lives in small flocks and moves around the bushes in secretive fashion. Appears like a miniature Brown-capped Babbler (*Pellorneum fuscocapillum*), except that it has a white throat. It prefers scrubland habitats and avoids thick forest. It is scattered throughout the island up to the mid hills and flocks are usually found in home gardens. Its call, a sharp *tchee-ik, chirik*, at times the elements uttered separately, indicates its presence.

Dark-fronted Babbler (Black-fronted Babbler)
Rhopocichla atriceps siccata 13 cm

Rukshan Jayewardene

A common bird throughout the island wherever wooded habitat is found. Three races have been described from the island with a race in the dry, wet and hill zones respectively. The pale eye contrasts with the dark forehead and black mask. Found in flocks in the shrub layer. Although not as loud as the other babblers, their calls are what usually betrays their presence: a hard *ch'k*, a prolonged *chrrrrr*, and a similar chatter. While feeding they work their way through tangled bushes and sometimes ascend trees.

* Orange-billed Babbler (Ceylon Rufous Babbler)
Turdoides rufescens 25 cm

T.S.U. de Zylva

(Endangered). Endemic. A fairly common species in and around the thick rain forests from the foothills to the mid hills, extending to suitable dense mountain forests in the higher hills. This noisy bird lives in flocks and is a regular species in bird waves. Their garrulous flocking habits makes them easy to observe and valuable for locating other birds. A flock maintains a flow of loud, chattering and squeaking sounds. When agitated, may utter loud laughing calls. Kitulgala and Sinharaja are the best places to see this species. At higher elevations, it is seen in Horton Plains NP and in the Peak Wilderness Sanctuary.

Yellow-billed Babbler (Southern Common Babbler)
Turdoides affinis taprobanus 23–24 cm

T.S.U. de Zylva

A common bird throughout the country up to the mid hills. Known as the 'Seven Sisters' on account of its habit of always being in a small flock. The flock is garrulous and its arrival in a garden is heralded by a chorus of calls: loud trills, squeaks, etc., some with a musical quality. It is a common garden bird. Avoids deep wet forest. Most members of the flock help build each nest, which may be shared.

* Ashy-headed Laughingthrush
Garrulax cinereifrons 23–24 cm

T.S.U. de Zylva

(Endangered). Endemic. A scarce species confined to thick rainforests in the foothills up to the higher hills. It lives in flocks and generally feeds and moves on or close to the ground. A flock utters a soft trill *chr, chrrr* mixed with soft short whistles. When agitated, may utter a laughing call. A regular species in bird waves in which they usually provide good views. Kitulgala and Sinharaja are very good sites for this species.

Great Tit (Grey Tit) *Parus major mahrattarum* 13–14 cm

The Sri Lankan race of Great Tit is over-all 'monochrome'-coloured. The call is clearly reminiscent of European race, but a distinct dialect. It is found through-out the island but is commoner in the hills. It is shy in the lowlands but much tamer in the hills. Often heard calls are *chirch-chee, chirrich-chee-wee* and *chirrit-ch'rr-ch'rr*, and it has dozens of additional calls and songs in its remarkably varied vocabulary. Lives in pairs but small flocks are not unusual. Male has broader black line down its underparts.

T.S.U. de Zylva

Velvet-fronted Nuthatch *Sitta frontalis* 11–13 cm

T.S.U. de Zylva

This attractive bird is found throughout the island wherever mature forest is found. In the dry zone it can be found especially on the tall mature Kumbuk trees that line the path of rivers. The species ascends high into the mountains and forms a part of the mixed feeding flocks that sweep through the forest. In typical nuthatch fashion, it descends head down along tree trunks. The call is a loud, very sharp *chik-chik-chik-chik* usually uttered together by both birds of a pair.

Purple-rumped Sunbird *Nectarinia zeylonica* 10–11 cm

T.S.U. de Zylva

T.S.U. de Zylva

(Left) *male;* (above) *female*

This little bird is a veritable garden jewel. The iridescent feathers on the male's purple rump contrast strongly with uniformly pale yellow underparts. Every garden in the suburbs of even the major towns appears to have its resident pair. Avoids the higher hills. All of the sunbirds build elaborate pear-shaped nests with a distinctive entrance roof over the entry hole. It is constructed from spider webs and other naturally occurring soft fibrous materials, and finished off with little chips of bark. The call is a high-pitched *tchwee* uttered once to three times, sometimes with slight variations. The male's song is a prolonged recital of sweet, high-pitched notes similar in tone to call.

Long-billed Sunbird (Loten's Sunbird)
Nectarinia lotenia 13–14 cm

T.S.U. de Zylva

This bird differs from similar Purple Sunbird (*Nectarinia asiatica*) by a longer and more curved beak, and calls. Female has brown upperparts and light underparts. Immature male similar to female but has dark stripe down the underparts. Found throughout the island but is commoner in the wet zone where it appears to replace Purple Sunbird. Its calls are high-pitched and somewhat 'metallic': while flying *chik, chik* and when perched *cheeuk*. The male's song consists mostly of a loud *chi-chichichichi* and a soft, clear *tee, tee-ti-ti* uttered alternately. Found only in south India and Sri Lanka.

Purple Sunbird *Nectarinia asiatica* 10–11 cm

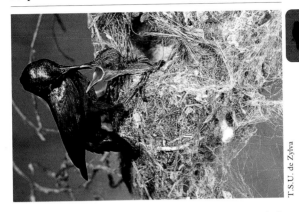

T.S.U. de Zylva

The male though dark overall is iridescent like other sunbirds. It is distinguished from Loten's by its beak which is short and slightly decurved, and calls. Found in the dry areas of the island up to mid hills. Female has brown upperparts and yellowish underparts, with a faint supercilium. Eclipse male similar to female but has dark stripe down the underparts. The call is a rather loud, high-pitched *tchreek, tchreek* and the male sings a loud song consisting of notes of similar quality with other sweeter notes.

* Legge's Flowerpecker *Dicaeum vincens* 10 cm

T.S.U. de Zylva

(Endangered). Endemic. A rather uncommon species in forests and adjoining gardens, around foothills and in the lower hills in wet zone. Lives in pairs and generally found high up on tall trees. The call is a sharp, rapid *kee-kee-kee-kee* pitched much higher than that of Pale-billed Flowerpecker (*Dicaeum erythrorhynchos*). Locating a male uttering its high-pitched song from a vantage point of a tall tree usually provides good views. The song is an ascending *keek-keek* ending with *tit-tiri-tit-tiri*. Sometimes found in bird waves. Bodhinagala, Kitulgala (e.g. Rest House garden), Gilimale, Morapitiya and Sinharaja are good places to see this species.

Pale-billed Flowerpecker (Tickell's Flowerpecker)
Dicaeum erythrorhynchos 8 cm

T.S.U. de Zylva

A common drab pale grey bird that is found throughout the island ascending to the highlands. Frequents the canopy of tall trees but common garden bird in the lowlands, where it will use TV antennas in residential areas as songposts. The calls are the familiar *tik, tik* and a clear, high-pitched trill *treee*. Song is a high-pitched *tirrr-tik-tik-tik-...* A very active bird, it flits around rapidly as it forages for food. It is fond of the berries of 'Jam trees' found in gardens. Often holds in its beak berries that are too large for it to swallow, and sucks the juice.

Oriental White-eye (Small White-eye)
Zosterops palpebrosa 10 cm

Eric Lott

A common bird in the lowlands found in both the dry and wet zones. It ascends the mid hills, but is rare above. It may be found in mixed flocks with Sri Lanka White-eye (*Zosterops ceylonensis*). It is a little smaller and yellower compared to the latter. Pairs or small flocks can be located by their constant soft medley of calls as they comb their way through the shrub layer searching for invertebrates. The commonest call is a soft, descending, anaemic *tveerr*. A short, pleasant song is of a similar tone. May also feed in the tops of low trees.

* Sri Lanka White-eye (Ceylon Hill White-eye)
Zosterops ceylonensis 11 cm

T.S.U. de Zylva

(Endangered). Endemic. A fairly common species in home gardens and forests in the higher hills. Occurs in small, and at times, large flocks which forage on tall trees as well as in low bushes. A nucleus species in bird waves. The soft chirping call is one of the most familiar in the higher hills: a short, cheerful *cheeyup* with a trilling quality, which has a few slight variations. In some areas it descends to forests in the lower hills as in Sinharaja where it mixes with Oriental White-eye (*Zosterops palpebrosa*). It is a little larger, and greener and darker than Oriental White-eye and has broader white eye-ring.

Black-hooded Oriole (Black-headed Oriole)
Oriolus xanthornus 24–25 cm

T.S.U. de Zylva

A common, widespread, garden and forest bird. It can be seen in the tree-lined streets of Colombo, but due to its habits of keeping to the tree tops, can be difficult to spot. The liquid flute-like calls give away its presence. One is *ku-kyi-ho* with the middle note higher than the other two, and sometimes the first note doubled. Other sounds include a sweet *chyowik* and a harsh *kuak*.

129

Brown Shrike *Lanius cristatus cristatus* 18–19 cm

T.S.U. de Zylva

A common migrant that occupies a number of habitats throughout the island. It can be seen in scrub adjoining marshes, village gardens, dry zone scrub forest and rainforest. Birds take up territories on arrival and advertise their presence with a limited vocabulary of unmusical call notes. It perches atop a bush scanning the ground vigilantly for prey, swooping down to catch its victims. Identified by the dark eye-mask and overall brown coloration. Juvenile shows barring on underparts and has a paler mask. The call when agitated is a distinctive, harsh chatter *tch-tch-tch-tch*.

Philippine Shrike *Lanius cristatus lucionensis* 18–19 cm

T.S.U. de Zylva

A subspecies of Brown Shrike (*Lanius cristatus cristatus*) from which it is distinguished by its clear grey crown, nape, hindneck and upper mantle. The commoner Brown can be mistaken for this race, but the grey on Philippine is very obvious. Scarce but regular visitor which may be overlooked for the commoner relative. Occurs throughout the island favouring bushy places from which it can sally out to catch prey.

White-bellied Drongo *Dicrurus caerulescens* 24 cm

A common bird from the lowlands to the mid hills. The only drongo to have white on the underparts. There are two races which are endemic to Sri Lanka. The wet zone form, White-vented (*leucopygialis*) has less white confined to the vent area. The dry zone form, White-bellied (*insularis*) has more white. Occurs in forest as well as suburbia. Its calls are loud, musical notes and chatterings. When agitated, it utters harsh notes. Drongos are good mimics and can imitate a number of birds and animals. It avoids the arid areas. Both races commonly use poles or wires as perches from which to catch prey.

T.S.U. de Zylva

Ceylon Crested Drongo *Dicrurus paradiseus lophorhinus* 35 cm

This race occurs in wet zone forests as the counterpart of Greater Racket-tailed Drongo (*Dicrurus paradiseus ceylonicus*) which occurs in dry zone forests. Generally, Ceylon Crested Drongo has a smaller and brush-like frontal crest and a deeply forked tail, without 'rackets'. In some birds (see plate), the crest can be as pronounced as in Racket-tailed race *ceylonicus*. The *lophorhinus* race is considered by some authors as a candidate to be split into a distinct species. The wet zone form is highly vocal and is easily located by its loud, bell-like calls and chatterings. It is a nucleus species in feeding flocks. It also has harsh calls, and mimics a variety of birds and a few animals.

T.S.U. de Zylva

131

Greater Racket-tailed Drongo *Dicrurus paradiseus ceylonicus*
33–35 cm (plus 30 cm tail)

Chew Yen Fook

A large, forest drongo. The 'racket-tailed' race *ceylonicus*, whose tail has the two long bare shafts with the ovoid feathers at the end, is found throughout the dry lowlands and is easily differentiated from the wet zone race *lophorhinus*. It has a large, distinctly back-curling frontal crest. Both races are endemic to Sri Lanka although this race is similar to that on mainland Asia. It is often seen in pairs. Riverine forests are a good place to locate it. Like all drongos it has wide repertoire of musical and bell-like notes.

Ashy Woodswallow (Ashy Swallow-shrike)
Artamus fuscus 19 cm

T.S.U. de Zylva

A rather uncommon resident that is often seen in pairs or small flocks perched on wires alongside roads. Can occur in lightly wooded areas but is most likely to be seen where it has a high vantage point over an open area to hunt for insects. Sometimes flies close to ground when hunting. In flight it has a 'swallow' shape, with triangular wings and square tail, and the darker face and throat contrasts with the paler underparts. It glides quite slowly. Its call is a nasal *cheek-cheek-cheek*.

*Sri Lanka Blue Magpie *Urocissa ornata* 42–47 cm

(Endangered). Endemic. A rather uncommon species confined to the wet zone, found in primary rainforest and sometimes in adjoining home gardens, from lowlands to higher hills. The rich-brown head and wings, blue body and red beak and legs are distinctive. Usually travels in pairs or in small, vocal flocks. The calls are loud and musical, some raucous. They include a rasping *cree-cree, cree-cree*, a ringing *ching, ching* and a plain, whistling *tlew-ee*. However, Ceylon Crested Drongo (*Dicrurus paradiseus lophorhinus*) found in same forests also gives similar calls. A rather shy member of the crow family, wary of humans, although will occur near forest villages and hermitages.

T.S.U. de Zylva

House Crow (Grey-necked Crow) *Corvus splendens* 40–42 cm

T.S.U. de Zylva

A common bird found in coastal areas and towns up to the lower hills. Its presence in large numbers is a natural response to the unsightly build up of rubbish dumps. Its notoriety as a lowly pest is unfortunate as crows are intelligent birds who show fascinating behaviour as individuals and as groups. House Crows are heavily parasitized by Asian Koel (*Eudynamys scolopacea*). The caw of this species is a rasping *kaaa*, weaker and a little longer than that of Large-billed Crow (*Corvus macrorhynchos*).

133

Large-billed Crow (Jungle Crow)
Corvus macrorhynchos 46–48 cm

T.S.U. de Zylva

Although it has a wide distribution, in towns it is not as abundant as House Crow (*Corvus splendens*) from which it can be distinguished by the absence of a grey neck and its bigger beak. Usually occurs as solitary individuals, or in twos and threes and does not form large flocks like House Crow. However, individuals of this species are often found within larger flocks of House Crows which gather at roosts or refuse dumps. In forested areas, this is the crow that is likely to be encountered. Its caw is a rasping *khaa*, stronger and deeper in tone than that of House Crow.

Brahminy Starling (Brahminy Myna)
Sturnus pagodarum 21–22 cm

T.S.U. de Zylva

An attractive ground-feeding bird, smaller than Common Myna (*Acridotheres tristis*). It has a long black crest which normally lies flat on the hindneck. It lives in flocks. Small flocks often feed on the ground while other birds perch nearby on small trees or bushes, and sing their long, soft, chattering song. Large flocks gather at a communal roost in the evening. It is a winter migrant from India and is found in coastal areas of the dry zone, mainly in the southeast. Small numbers are occasionally found in the wet zone, apparently on their way to their usual dry zone habitats. Its song is a continuous medley of chirps, croaks and squeaks.

Rosy Starling (Rose-coloured Starling)
Sturnus roseus 21–24 cm

A beautiful bird when it is in pink and black breeding plumage. In non-breeding plumage it becomes duller. Most of the time in Sri Lanka, it is found in drab non-breeding plumage. Immature is brown. In all of these plumages, yellow on the lower mandible is distinct. Generally occurs in flocks, feeding both on trees and on the ground. Large numbers gather to roost communally and sometimes share roosts with flocks of Brahminy Starling (*Sturnus pagodarum*). It is a winter migrant to coastal areas of the dry zone, mainly to the southeast. An irruptive species; numbers fluctuate annually. Occasionally found in the wet zone, usually on passage. Birds gathering at roosts utter a soft continuous twittering.

T.S.U. de Zylva

Common Myna *Acridotheres tristis* 24 cm

T.S.U. de Zylva

One of the commonest birds in the country, certainly where the landscape is under human influence. It may be seen scavenging in the scrap heaps in towns although its diet is mainly insects. It nests in tree holes but is largely a terrestrial bird of open ground. Although it has adapted well to humans, its relative lack of abundance in the cities may be due to a lack of nesting holes being a limiting factor. However, cities may have large roosts. It makes a variety of familiar loud, chattering or squeaking calls, the one most often heard being *kak-kak, kyok-kyok-kyok-kyok, tchiyu-tchiyu-tchiyu*, with each phrase higher in pitch.

135

Southern Hill Myna *Gracula indica* 25 cm

T.S.U. de Zylva

The form of Hill Myna found in Sri Lanka and southwest India has been recently described as a 'good' species and split from *religiosa* into a new species Southern Hill Myna (*Gracula indica*). In Sri Lanka, it is largely confined to the wet zone ascending to the mid hills. Its range overlaps with endemic Sri Lanka Myna (*Gracula ptilogenys*) where there is thick forest. From the latter it is distinguished by the double pair of head wattles with one below the eye and the lack of black on the base of the bill. The call is a loud penetrating long-drawn *keeeyu*.

House Sparrow *Passer domesticus indicus* 15 cm

T.S.U. de Zylva

A familiar town and garden bird, that will readily take up residence in clay pots that are put up as nest boxes. It is found throughout the island, close to human habitation. The male is more brightly coloured and has a grey cap. The female is nondescript with a distinct pale supercilium. Occurs in small flocks outside the breeding season. Its chirps and cheeps can be heard even in heavily built-up areas. Its numbers have recently declined.

136

Streaked Weaver (Striated Weaver) *Ploceus manyar* 14–15 cm

T.S.U. de Zylva

A colony of nesting weavers is easily betrayed by the screeching song and general activity of the males that seems to be part of its social life. This species nests in reeds or low bushes standing in water. The nest is a dome without the long funnel woven by Baya Weaver (*Ploceus philippinus*). Restricted to the dry lowlands, it is less abundant than Baya Weaver, with which it is frequently found in lakeside reeds. Distinguished from Baya by the heavily streaked underparts and lack of any yellowish tinge on the underparts.

Baya Weaver *Ploceus philippinus* 15 cm

T.S.U. de Zylva

A common bird in the dry lowlands, where large flocks may ravage crops. Local in wet zone. Frequently found in mixed flocks with Streaked Weaver (*Ploceus manyar*) although Baya prefers more open country habitat. Female duller than male and lacks yellow on male's crown. The song of the male, often uttered from the half-completed nest, consists of prolonged chattering and squeaks, some of them drawn-out. The domed nests with a funnel appear a work of supreme craftsmanship; a single tree may hold many such nests.

137

Indian Silverbill
Euodice malabarica 10–11 cm

Indian Silverbill is an uncommon dry zone species. In Sri Lanka it is mainly found in the very dry stretch around the northern peninsula and the adjacent coastal strips. It is also found in the dry areas of the south. Found in pairs or in small flocks. May mix in flocks with other munias. The overall impression is of small, elegant bird with a long pointed tail. A white rump contrasts with the pale brown upperparts, otherwise it is fairly nondescript. The call is a soft *tchirip*.

White-rumped Munia
Lonchura striata 10–11 cm

Quite unmistakable in its two-tone plumage. The white rump contrasts strongly with the blackish-brown upperparts and wings. The juvenile is duller but shares the two-tone pattern of the adult. It is found throughout the country, except for the dry northernmost areas, and ascends up to the mountains. It usually travels in small flocks, foraging in grasslands and paddy fields. It often visits home gardens. The calls are a clear *tweet, tweet*, usually uttered in flight, and a soft *trrrp*.

Scaly-breasted Munia (Spotted Munia)
Lonchura punctulata 11–12 cm

T.S.U. de Zylva

A common bird found throughout the island, ascending to the highlands where it may be seen in the same habitat as the endemic Black-throated Munia (*Lonchura kelaarti*). The latter has a distinctly black face. The upperparts are a brighter brown and underparts have black scales against white, different to the bolder black 'arrow heads' against white of Black-throated. It forages on grasslands and crops, and is regarded as a pest. It constructs large, untidy, dome-shaped nests on trees and will move into gardens to occupy suitable nesting habitats. In cities, flocks may descend to wasteland, but the restless flocks seldom stay in one place for long. The call is a soft squeaky *peep*.

Black-headed Munia *Lonchura malacca* 11 cm

T.S.U. de Zylva

The deep black head and chestnut upperparts easily separate this species from other munias. It occurs throughout the island, mainly in the dry zone in grasslands and marshlands. Its presence on paddy fields is not welcomed but its relatively low numbers do not make it as much of a pest as Scaly-breasted Munia (*Lonchura punctulata*). Juvenile is nondescript dull brown and could be confused with juvenile of commoner Scaly-breasted Munia. From the latter it can be separated by the heavy silvery-blue bill.

139

Glossary

Barring Lines 'sideways' on a bird, such as on the tail or breast. Lines lengthwise are referred to as streaking.

Chestnut Reddish-brown.

Coverts A group of feathers that cover a certain part of the bird, for example the ear coverts, undertail coverts etc.

Dry zone The part of Sri Lanka which receives relatively little rain due to the interaction of the two monsoons with the topography of the country. In particular the central mountain massif influences the distribution of rainfall. The dry zone comprises all of the island outside the wet south-west quadrant.

Eclipse A duller plumage assumed by the males of certain species following breeding, when males often resemble females. Eclipse plumage is a common feature of ducks.

Feeding flock A flock of birds, usually comprising several different species which forage collectively, utilising different parts of the habitat as they pass through it.

Feral Escaped from captivity and now living in a wild state.

Gape The corner of the mouth where the upper and lower mandibles meet. In certain birds like the Great Egret the gape line is an identification feature.

Good species Usually refers to a bird that was formerly considered a race, but now 'split' as a separate species.

Intermediate zone A zone that is transitional between the wet and dry zones. It has its own flora, and its bird life shares characteristics with that of both the dry and wet zones.

Iris, plural **Irides** The part of the eye around the pupil, which corresponds to the coloured part of the human eye.

Jizz A combination of characteristics of a bird that enables an experienced birdwatcher to identify a species even if a good look is not obtained. This can be a combination of habitat, the profile and posture of a bird, its behaviour and any other subtle but useful clues to its identity.

Local Refers to a 'patchy' distribution within a region.

Lores The part between a bird's beak and eye. In some birds (e.g. egrets) the lores are bare skin which changes colour with breeding condition. Some birds have a 'loreal', line which is a useful identification feature.

Lump To treat two or more forms previously regarded as distinct species as races of a single species.

Mantle A cloak-like covering of feathers formed by the feathers on the upper back and the scapulars. Sleeping birds often tuck their head under the mantle.

Morph A distinct colour form (pale, dark etc.) occurring within a single population of a bird.

Nuchal crest A crest that falls along the back of the neck.

Primaries The outermost nine to eleven flight feathers on the wing of a bird.

Race or **subspecies** A diagnosably different population of a species, which is geographically separated from the rest of the species.

Scapulars A group of feathers that cover the base of the wing and the shoulders.

Secondaries The inner flight feathers on the wing of a bird.

Speculum A rectangle of colour on the outer secondaries. Especially useful in the identification of ducks.

Split A term used to describe dividing what have been considered the races of one species into separate species.

Stake-out A term used by birders to refer to a site, such as a roost, which is a reliable place to see a particular species of bird.

Supercilium The technical term for an 'eye-brow' formed by feathers of a different colour.

Tertials In some birds the innermost secondaries (i.e. closest to the body) are elongated and are referred to as tertials.

Wet zone The part of Sri Lanka which receives heavy rain due to the interaction of the two monsoons with the topography of the country. This is comprised largely of the south-western sector of the country and the central mountain massif.

Wewa A man made lake. There are hundreds of these in the dry zone of Sri Lanka. Many are centuries old and are bound in history.

Wingbar A band of colour on the wing formed by feathers having a different colour to the surrounding feathers. The presence or absence of a wingbar may be an important identification feature, especially with waders.

Useful addresses

If you are interested in Sri Lankan birds, consider membership of the following local organisations.

Ceylon Bird Club, 39, Chatham Street, Colombo 1.
Tel 328625/7. Fax 075 332394. E-mail: birdclub@sltnet.lk

Wildlife and Nature Protection Society (WNPS), 86, Rajamalwatta Road, Battaramulla. Tel 887390. Fax 887664

Field Ornithology Group of Sri Lanka (FOGSL), Department of Zoology, University of Colombo, Colombo 3.
Fax 337644. E-mail: fogsl@slt.lk

For a wider perspective consider membership of the following:

Oriental Bird Club, The Lodge, Sandy, Beds, SG19 2DL, UK.
Website: http://www.orientalbirdclub.org/

Index

142

144